The Poetry Review

The Poetry Society, 22 Betterton Street, London WC2H 9BX

The Poetry Review

The Poetry Society, 22 Betterton Street, London WC2H 9BX
Tel: +44 (0)20 7420 9883 • Fax: +44 (0)20 7240 4818
Email: poetryreview@poetrysociety.org.uk
www.poetrysociety.org.uk

Editor: Maurice Riordan
Production: Michael Sims

ISBN: 978-1-900771-89-4 ISSN: 0032 2156
Cover illustration Sarah Hanson / Début Art

. . .

SUBMISSIONS
For details of our submission guidelines, please visit the *The Poetry Review* section of www.poetrysociety.org.uk

ADVERTISING
To advertise, visit poetrysociety.org.uk or contact Robyn Donaldson on +44 (0)20 7420 9886, email: marketing@poetrysociety.org.uk

BOOKSHOP DISTRIBUTION
Central Books, 99 Wallis Road, London E9 5LN, UK. Tel: 0845 458 9925 or visit www.centralbooks.com

PBS EXCLUSIVE BOOK SUPPLY SERVICE
Readers of *The Poetry Review* can receive many of the books featured in the magazine post-free by mail order from the Poetry Book Society. To order, tel: +44 (0)20 7831 7468, Mon-Fri, quoting *The Poetry Review.*

SUBSCRIPTIONS & SALES
UK individuals: £34 / Europe: £44
Rest of the World: £49
(all overseas delivery is by airmail)
Single issue: £8.95 plus postage.
Order from www.poetryreview.org.uk or contact Paul McGrane on +44 (0)20 7420 9881.
Pay by cheque (sterling and US dollar cheques only), credit card or Direct Debit.

The Poetry Review is also available on audio CD.

The Poetry Review is the magazine of the Poetry Society and was first published in 1912. A subscription to *The Poetry Review* is included as part of membership of the Poetry Society. It is also available from leading bookshops. Views expressed in *The Poetry Review* are not necessarily those of the Poetry Society; those of individual contributors are not necessarily those of the Editor.

Charity Commission No. 303334

CONTENTS

Poems

Prose

Poems

Reviews

The Geoffrey Dearmer Prize 2014

EDITORIAL

'The Love Song of J. Alfred Prufrock' was published a hundred years ago in the June issue of *Poetry*. T.S. Eliot appeared unremarked alongside poets who were, according to the editor Harriet Monroe, "well known to our readers". It is alarming, at least for me, to come across their names now: Bliss Carman? Skipwith Cannell? Arthur Davison Ficke? Carman survives as a historical figure in Canadian poetry. Cannell, it turns out, was a friend of Ezra Pound and a well respected imagist, whose lyrics today indicate the shelf-life of the movement.

Ficke's contribution is a sequence of dreadful sonnets in memory of Rupert Brooke, who had died in April (from "sunstroke", according to the editor). Ficke, though, remains the interesting one, remembered for his part as Anne Knish in the *Spectra* hoax. This anthology of modernist "experiments" would come out in 1916 complete with a spoof manifesto: "a poem is to be regarded as a prism, upon which the colorless white light of infinite existence falls and is broken up into glowing, beautiful, and intelligible hues... The rays which the poet has dissociated into colorful beauty should recombine in the reader's brain into a new intensity of unified brilliance." It hoodwinked the editors of the day.

Meanwhile, 'Prufrock' had sprung from the pages of *Poetry* fully formed in its modernity. Younger poets are currently cultivating a vogue for pastiche, bathos, collage, the conceit, the self mummified in layers of irony. But here it all was – in the unlocated voice, the bits of Marvell and *Hamlet*, the heterogeneous ideas "yoked" together, the daring aplomb with which the yellow fog

> Let fall upon its back the spot [sic] that falls from chimneys,
> Slipped by the terrace, made a sudden leap,
> And seeing that it was a soft October night,
> Curled once about the house, and fell asleep.

Eliot's modernism had its roots in late nineteenth-century affluence. Its backdrop is a cosmopolitan lifestyle of incandescent lighting, arcades, crowds, terrorism, smog, social anxiety. A century on and some of those furnishings have changed. The concepts of alienation, solipsism and ennui, it seems, have not – or not yet.

But poets are restive animals. Once again we see them roaming widely, as you will find especially in the prose of this issue: Flarf, Alt Lit, et al. They are on the hunt for new ways to ironise the self, as well as old ways to tap into the spirit: ellipsis, parataxis, syntaxis, transgressive lineation, anything perhaps to rend the veil of the temple. It's rough weather for sonnet and villanelle, but wonderful times for a magazine to be the conduit of such energy, and to act as an arena for so much competitive and diverse activity.

Treacherous as well: it's all too easy to mistake the outmoded for the old-fashioned, or miss the genuinely new amid the merely novel. Some of the most exciting developments will vanish, as did pneumatic post and O'Shaughnessy's Indian Telegraph. Over time the shyly inventive, the slyly subversive, or the stubbornly low-key, may thrive. We may be in prime territory, too, for a hoax.

Maurice Riordan

SARA PETERS

Black Box

We were born knowing nothing of our bodies
except that we needed to discard them, and after
years of subjecting these bodies to reckless
gymnastics, frequent, deliberately contracted
illnesses, general lack of plenitude, and
nonspecific sorrow, at last it was our turn to
rappel down the cliff.

Rope shot through our hands. Something burned
behind us – not the house – and we were weary,
bent necks topped with withered faces, our flesh
in ghastly shambles. Some of us were so empty
we billowed, some of us had shoulders rubbed to
nearly nothing by the backpacks we carried.

Who had seen us before? Various tellers,
conductors and bakers. The moths in our clothes,
the mice in our walls. We peeled our dinner from
the rocks at the shore, we were prepared to stay,
we'd wait. French-braided Elizabeth, naked beneath
a mohair blanket, the insane uncle, in flip-flops
and gold splash pants – a modest person, whose
only goal was to have sex with God – under the
slight, wet wind we tended first to our fires, then
only to our breathing, as we marked the arrival of
nothing and no one.

That night we all lay in the tent, watching the
bodies of insects in shadow cross over its skin,
until we all dropped into the same sickened dream.
For all this time we'd thought the sensation of
living was a hand at our throat in a grip that was

ours to loosen, once we reached the shore – for all these years we'd held the belief that we'd been designed for this journey, that we were worth being greeted at the end of it by faceless beings who would approach from all sides, pull the pins from our limbs and our hair, work the knots from our back, and lay upon us, with nearly unbearable tenderness, dozens of hands –

The Stages of Harriet

Harriet was given no love of any kind, for the townspeople wanted a mystic, and they thought they could create one through torture. They believed that a mystic would bring spiritual complexity to their Town – the same thinking that often leads rich westerners to take up Buddhism in later life. The townspeople chose Harriet, and then subtracted shelter, and affection. Education had never been part of the question, and sex, they imagined, would take care of itself. She was kept in a stable, fed raw flour and fallen fruit, and made to drink water from a hose. Her desire to make jokes at her own expense was crushed, for it was a suspect quality, in such a young person. And then, one April, Harriet was let loose unsupervised in a field.

She parcelled out her time building homes for herself under trees – this life was not that different from the life that was normally hers. Burrowing moles left behind small packets of grass, which she collected and formed into beds for the animals she thought might approach. Meanwhile, the townspeople produced a yellowish, oniony sweat, their eyes bulged with concentration, as they worked day and night to not love her. Individual successes were rewarded: who could see, in a telescope as in a dream, the girl shivering as she slept beneath bark, and refrain from wincing? Who could bear to watch her try to remove her lips and eyelashes, which she had been told were purely decorative, and not interfere?

A river ran by Harriet's field. Once she saw a child, attended by two women in haltertops that featured reindeer kicking up showers of sequin snowflakes. The women held the child up by her armpits and skimmed her feet lightly across the surface of the water, barely wetting her soles. *God bless you,* the child said to Harriet, having spotted her. The women stopped their swinging: *Who?* That night, Harriet built a bed for this child, too. Later that week, animals finally approached but they did not sniff Harriet lightly and then, overwhelmed by her innocence and purity of heart, depart. The townspeople watched the encounter in their telescopes; they could not reach her slowly enough. They wove toward her with wonder and delight, as if moving through close-set trees toward a sudden, sourceless waterfall.

Harriet was later sealed like a gumball in a clear plastic globe and suspended over the Town square, while everyone waited to see if the skin grafts would take hold. The skin of her thighs became the skin of her cheeks, the skin of her back newly coated her front. Strangely, she indeed became a mystic, but not the right type, for her sense of humour bubbled back up, and her attempts to traverse between spiritual planes typically ended in broken hands and feet, and ever more delicate surgeries. Harriet went about her calling with a steady cheer that the townspeople found both admirable and appalling. She would rise in the morning and not even take coffee before flinging herself over and over again at the spiked and burning veil between the worlds.

Hating Men

I remember when my daughter began to hate men. The river outside of the room she slept in was now choked with them; they floated downstream without struggling, their football jerseys or suits and ties or loose yoga clothing partly torn off and trailing behind them. Demolished, crushed, vanishing men. My daughter had been supplied, early in her life, with a narrow white cat that sat like an icicle in her doorframe, guarding her room, and this cat appeared to hate men, too, though it was itself male. It hissed and spat when my husband or any of his brothers or friends entered my daughter's room.

The first time I noticed my daughter actively hating men she was six, and we were in a grocery store. It is important to know that earlier in the day a customer had smashed a bottle of rosemary and peppermint shampoo. A young man, a teenager, walked by wheeling a cart full of radishes. His blockish white smock and blockish white shoes appeared to have been constructed from the same material, and the front of his smock was stained with what must have been butcher's blood, though my daughter openly speculated.

Passing by us the young man bared his teeth at my daughter in a lascivious way seconds before stepping on the shampoo puddle, slipping backwards and cracking his head on the concrete floor, his teeth vanishing back into his mouth,

and the cart tipping backwards on top of him,
hundreds of radishes rolling out and gradually
covering his fallen body like petals.

The second time that my daughter's true and everlasting hatred of men surfaced was at a museum, when she saw a sculpture of Penthesilea, the Amazon queen, disembowelling one of Odysseus's men. My daughter, nine by now, started clapping when she glimpsed it from sixty feet, and clapped louder and faster the closer we got.

There were multiple instances of open man-hating during my daughter's teenage years, but the one I recall with the greatest clarity happened in early fall after she had been taken by a friend to a lavender field that they had planned to pillage and use to stuff pillowettes. This friend, female of course, was treacherous: she outwardly sympathised with my daughter's man-hating ways, while plotting against her in secret. They roamed the field for fewer than fifteen minutes before men began to pop out from behind trees – members of her co-ed volleyball team, the treacherous friend told my daughter.

Later, my daughter decided she didn't want to attend college, but when subjected to an avalanche of criticism (mostly, I am sad to say, from me) she relented, and chose a school that admitted only women. Being my man-hating daughter she lasted one semester only and appeared home in December to tell me that there had been a mixer with the 'sibling college' several miles down the road. My daughter claimed to have miniaturised several hundred men from this mixer and smuggled them home in a jumbo bottle of Robaxacet. She did this, she told me, in order to observe their behaviour under stress.

I avoided checking in on the laboratory that her room gradually became, and I can only assume that those experimented-upon men are the same men currently clogging our river; that once my daughter has completed her tests she crushes them quietly, returns them to size, and places them (perhaps with unaccountable tenderness?) in the water, so that they may pass quietly to some other side, arms crossed, like many hundreds of Ladies of Shalott.

Hooves

She left me, walking away through fields of carrots and corn. I recalled every time I had embarrassed myself in her presence, been dirty, sick, stupid and drunk, and I wanted to reel all those memories back into myself, though I knew they would corrode me, for I was not like her, with a mind like a typesetter's drawer. At first, the townspeople brought offerings: sugary wine and chocolates of obscure flavor: pine, rosemary, pavement-after-summer-rain. They brought these things because they were desperate, for I was the only doctor, though I had none of the qualities you might expect: clear eyes, strong hands, an abstract commitment to humanity. For days after she left me, I persevered, neatened my eyebrows, screwed on earrings, placed drops in my eyes, but I was too frightened to open my door. Townspeople gathered outside my windows, five deep at each pane, thinner every day, their jewellery tarnishing. Meanwhile ferns refurled, light snow whirled down, and I could hear the soft wood of my house giving way. At every turn I felt my brain's black rot slosh in my skull. I woke to the sound of some foreign sea in my ear.

And so I ran. At first, I took the path she'd walked to leave me. I ran into new seasons, new ages. I ran till my hooves wore down completely, then I wobbled on stumps. The townspeople and their ailments, their cancers and pregnancies, nearly forgotten. My loyalty only to myself, even though I'd discarded my name. I staggered on my kneecaps, I had grown very thin, and yet if I balanced at a certain angle my features were not unbeautiful to me. I moved through old lands, old industries. What was left of my legs contained much impacted material: gravel and dirt, but also cigarette butts, take-out spoons, pennies and French fries and dimes all driven up into the flesh, but the real humour came when I wore myself down to my pelvis. I laughed as I rolled forth, but not the laughter you're imagining: black, deranged, torn; it was the laughter of a good-natured person who has jogged into a telephone pole. I gave myself over to feats of concentration: how long could I live with this stick in my eye, with my neck at this angle? I had always been a clean woman, and luckily in the later months the rain kept me in the manner to which I was accustomed. And then one hour I found myself subjected to a vision. At this point summer was collapsing into fall and I had worn myself down to my ribcage, yet still I rolled forth.

In this vision my body had been refurbished, and I came to a field of bluebells and stood just at the edge, for I could no more imagine trampling the flowers than I could imagine trampling a field of human faces. I stood just at the edge of this field, and townspeople began to appear in a circle around it, each one healthy and well-tended, as if, in my absence, they had taken their bodies into their own hands. I felt a luxurious contentment in this, as we all drew closer, this makeshift community, and noticed the banked glow of our skins. But I was torn early from this vision, before it could bring me true comfort or clarity. I woke alone at the end of a suburban driveway, having worn myself down to my broad shoulders, which during the course of my journey I had come to love, if only because they resembled hers, which I remembered in detail: specifically how they looked in her sweater, as she walked away.

DALJIT NAGRA

The Love Song of Mugoo and Gugoo

Mugoo was a sweeper boy and the cleanest
of the sweeper caste. He would leap at the blush
of dawn to clean the paths and the steps spotless.

Gugoo was a bootmaker girl who made boots.
Gugoo was higher caste than Mugoo. By rights
this should have been the end of their contact.

In the after-work, while the boys and girls played
at tug of war, wrestling or archery, shy boy Mugoo
and shy girl Gugoo would draw the boys and girls.

The children smiling at the shining visions would hug
Mugoo and Gugoo. Then that couple would ablaze
the drawings for fear their elders feel scandalised.

In manhood for Mugoo and womanhood for Gugoo,
how hard that Gugoo thread boots for her father
when she had no golden stitch for the gaping hole

in her soul. How hard that Mugoo mop the lanes!
Who dare be swept away from the law of caste
by the foul stamp and passport of besotted love?

Yet the hairs at their ears, their nipples, bomped
by a mere sultana breeze. Then the swirling night
when they'd escape for Arabia than stay near-far...

In Mugoo and Gugoo Love was a rabbit leaping on
a mooli when they became runaway lovers! Like hares
under the sketched moon they bobbed in the grunch

wind before the monster'd river. Timorous Gugoo
to timorous Mugoo, 'Is it not said the pure of heart
are able to turn water into solid crystal orbs?'

'I have heard it, Gugoo. Let us swim till the waters
turn dot by dot into crystal orbs – slowly mounting
up for us a solid path so we can bobble across.'

That cub-like couple gave each other a first daredevil
ever cuddle. Then snuck a tiny kiss! And fell into
their dive across old Punjab's wide grumbling ogre –

the river Ravi! They were soon to learn the blunderous
water was bigger than they; they were dabbing onwards
on the spot; directionless comical pups; pawdawdling...

Only Death was woken by their swallowed screams.
At the sight of a harmless pair brinked for his maw
Death's pink lips aah'd and coo'd. To tickle himself

Death tipped a lambing moan in the eardrums
of the ferryman, Charan, who was rank in a dream.
Charan swore at Death, 'What bastard *panchod*

is unheroing my dream? I was the River-God –
when I was riding on the river the fisher king's
red bill was fishing me a buxom masala mermaid!'

Death hushed Charan. Bundled him into the boat.
Charan, still swearing, fished for a scream-trail,
for bunny-like feet in the sudden dead-stop river...

Next morning, by the prophecy of the snake-priest
the villagers arrived at the shame-faced riverbank.
Charan, in his sgruggy lilac turban, was blaring

at the crowd about a passion-crime. Huffing too
had arrived the muscly cobbler and sweeper fathers.
All heard Charan, 'I am my own King of the Sticks!

I row two weeks that way to the flowers of Kashmir
floating men back with their bloated bags of honey,
and another week that way toward the Arabian spices

from where the traders return with kalonji and jeera.
Today I sing you my parable, my moral, my allegory
and blessing. Is it costing you even a *panchod* rupee?'

And there by Charan's sandal'd feet, amid his din,
quietly shivering and wrapped in the same brave
blanket (like a chapatti rolled around saag-paneer)

yet fearing to be parted, yet tenuously panting were
Mugoo and Gugoo! The frail couple like shy red
squirrels, 'O father, we love you. But. Most we are...

loving this: this that is my soul's mirror. Mugoo is
my Gugoo: Gugoo is my Mugoo.' The bony youths
clung sauced together. Stiffed for the glooping apart.

The bootmaker father been crunching his own fists,
the sweeper father been hurling daggers from his eyes,
as the crowd fell silent, heard their dearly beloveds

whispering again, in the apricot breeze, 'Do not...
part us.' Of sweet-faced Mugoo in his threadbare voice,
of sweet-faced Gugoo in her threadbare voice,

whose words had risen like the song of love in a breeze
swooning the hills and valleys into heavens of blossom,
surely no power on earth would ever part such wonder...

The Dream of Mr Bulram's English

i

From chalk face to the latest newfangled screen
I remain an English teacher before my shades-
of-the-globe teenagers. With a click I summon
imperishable lines from our island and from abroad
for their marriage between sense and mellifluous
sentence, for the way they've jazzed our lexicon.
My awesome role's to grade but also to inspire
each teen with a lust for our courtly vowels.

ii

I pray they'll honour this tongue William dared
never to conquer, for who dare battle against
an autochthonous force! I hope to spin their minds
timeless with Chaucer, Donne, Keats and Byron,
with Tennyson and Browning. And lead them across
the spellbound shores of our tongue Shakespearean
rousing oration into stately cadence till it one day
fight on the beaches in that tongue Churchillian.

iii

If some students in the double lessons feel trapped,
if this tongue feels a curse, this flesh feels too solid
without, if this language feels ill-begot so its terms
cause shame, if we're still at sea with the whip-hand's
lashing tongue, if we're still at sea and the margin's
fading... How can we thrive in the West unless we hear,
for better or worse, the link with our distant ancestors:
this heartfelt Word, evermore, this shared tongue?

iv

Our ancestors took on the grand dreams of the King
James Bible and grafted the English canon. I respect
the hurt but we're now in the main, now that thought
in this tongue springs universal. I wish my students peace
in a word so dignity reign. I wish them Martin Luther
King's imposing marble mimicry and free speech
steering its own course through the ruling demesne
to imply this lingua franca has become our lineage.

v

Why live in a tongue you'd hurt – you'd mercenary
grab the rules to bend, as if the migrant past justified
an offshore narrative of high-tech fast-talk portfolios...
If my class tread on water and arrive at the isthmus
of poetry they'll find they're enshrined in high art,
they've a stake worth the investment! So I bless them
the passion of Wordsworth who saved and saved
simply to behold a canvas-bound Arabian Nights.

JAMIE COWARD

Peasholm Park

Now it wears the backlot's so-what look
as props are hauled from set to set,
painted up or stored in sheds for winter.
The shinto bridge is padlocked shut.
The island can't be reached again this year.
A good moment for end credits
but before the first words can appear,
the mind, hardwired for magic,
must dissolve to a summer evening:
voices, various sources of music,
the lake seen from the island,
lights melting on the water
then the sky framed with a flourish
by the roof of the pagoda.

The Mist

Even as we move towards the mist
on Kinder Scout we are no more
than two miles and a shout from roads.
But as the mist closes around us
there is an exchange of looks.
No map. No compass.
Then the disembodied sound
of a helicopter, not far above us
though it could be in another world,
one overlapped by this,
where some disaster has occurred.

STEPHEN KNIGHT

Sh

Leaving these unloved rooms
  The dark is welcome to,
  Leaving these dark blue
Shadowy walls

Leaving softly, slowly through
  Unlocked doors, and there!
  Toys beyond repair
Torturing the floor

Leaving empty every chair
  Because it must be right
  To forfeit *if* and *might*
Then hurry off

Leaving before daylight
  Topples across the bed,
  Even before my head
Gives up its dreams.

MARY ROBINSON

You asked for a poem about listening
for Kathryn

How easy is it to represent a sound in words?
Take, for example, the sound of a dog's paws

on frozen leaves – a medium-sized dog – and notice
how the pads spread apart. The leaves are stiff
and the ice crystals abrade each other.
The dog does not press down hard with his feet.
As he walks a few grains of frost cling
to his paws. When he runs he disturbs the leaves
so that they have a right side (frosted)
and an underside (unfrosted) like scraps
of satin cloth. The dog's breath steams
in the chill air. Far off to the south-east
dawn burns. A heron studies the river.
Soon rooks will rise from their roost to begin
a day's forage in the fields. And the sound? Crunch
is too sharp (boots walking on gravel). Crack –
no, that's pine resin in the fire. Snap –
worse still – twigs, not leaves, under the same boots.

It's the sound of movement on a still morning,
the sound of a dog's paws on frozen leaves.

MILES BURROWS

The Crocodile-skin Handbag

Thick scales glisten below the Adam's apple
And on the arms. I'm slowly changing
Into a crocodile. Like something out of Ovid.
I am changing into Mum's crocodile-skin handbag,
Expensive but completely out of fashion,
Always upstairs when it should be downstairs
('It must be downstairs darling, could you look?')
Impossible to find at the last moment. ('Maddening.
I must have left it upstairs – it's too hectic.')
I longed to be that handbag
Centre of perpetual attention
So elusive and effortlessly maddening
Able to be upstairs and downstairs at once
And suddenly to manifest on Mum's lap all the time.
In old age, the crocodile-skin handbag
Waits hiding on her lap beneath the table.
And at supper, with an actor's smile,
She slips fresh scampi into its open mouth
To give later to the cat.

Four Last Things

1. You will have time enough to sleep.
So get some practice now, you always need more.
Hold onto the penis tightly like
The stopper on a lukewarm hot water bottle.
The other hand should be clenched in a fist over your mouth.
Relax and think of the happy times
You might have had.

2. In Berlin for example. Somewhere you have never been.
You would surely have enjoyed it. In Berlin.
Eating German food. The hearty breakfasts.
You could have lived in Kantstrasse
And gone to work on a tram.
You could surprise people
By speaking words in German as you die.

3. Or slip into Old Slavonic at the last.
Ask for *shchee*.
That'll give them a shock.
They'll come with banners and hampers,
Black headscarves, *pirozhki*,
Through the snow, out of the forest: sledges, horses' breath steaming
in the cold air.

4. Afterwards, old men in felt-lined boots
Will walk back into the woods, taking snuff, talking about billiards.

GRAHAM MORT

La Maison Bleue

Before I died, we rented a blue house
on a narrow street that twisted down
to a river bridge's leaping arch.

The house had photographs of a family
just like mine: the parents happy back
in time, looking sideways to the future,

their children born into a Technicolor
age that left them fading from walls: all
handmade brick, lime render and stone

the tincture of honey or that quaint
gesture – a curl of hair in a silver locket.
Since the house was finished in oak, I

thought of my coffin in a black car, my
grown-up children by the graveside, a
baby I'd never know in someone's arms.

At night we left a casement open and
a bat flew in, its echolocation bouncing
from the angles of the room: I could

see it as a cat's cradle (that old
marmalade Tom chancing the dusk)
or a parable with many meanings.

When I woke it was under a heavy quilt:
a smell of mice, the sharp sounds of
birds in our fig trees, the river tugging

its fish to face the current, ants at
their labour, a lizard growing a new
tail. There was a market in the

square, a bodhrán's solemn pulse
making it Sunday. When I reached
for a glass of water my fingerprints

were magnified and white and very
bright. There was a dark stain on
the coverlet, the vine outside glowing

green as if sap was flame. You were
saying something about the heat –
still sleepy, still beautiful – shuffling

into a summer skirt of dark blue
plums; my shoes on the floor, their
footprints heading somewhere.

Pigeonnier

He walks through a cloud of blue moths –
    one for each apostle – into a round tower

with a peaked *chapeau* of tiles, the oak door
    rotted, wasps fierce in the vine, limestone

steps hollowed. Rows of nesting boxes dark
    as the eyes of city whores; pigeons sleeping;

a wedge of sun chiselling mica through dusky
    air. Now the quiet clamour of roosting birds

kept for the eggs he candles in the sacristy;
    for the sweet meat of their breasts and dung

dug into the Abbé's onion beds; for music of
    a sort: the crooning of forbidden sex, blood

bubbling from a man's cut throat. The boy
    reaches to their stink, peering at novices

working the pump below: their creamy thighs
    and sleek-dipped heads, their oxter hair and

sideways looks; soapy laughter, stiff nipples,
    wide eyes and slender hands. Now this back-

plumage black as smeared soot; iridescent
    necks; this underwing down dense with heat

and lice and suffocating dark. Their amber
    eyes stare incuriously as he kills, wringing

out last sobs of life, lining them up neat
    as martyrs cut down from a cross of air.

JENNIFER L. KNOX

Sakura Matsuri

Bleached police ghosts come about day three
if you're one of those *Can't complain!* SOBs.
Day one for the restless rest of us, gnashing
and kicking ourselves to sleep. Jesus just makes
us sadder. And watching you bust your hump
loving Jesus? Jesus. He took one for the team
but his bearded handlers are bad mofos.
The trees are blooming furiously, Incredible
Hulk style, blossoms swan-diving into the abyss.
We should be blissed out on a tropical island
eating fake fish shaped like a party steak.
After a long night bowing deeply in dreams,
a thought: 'I'm good at this!' The song
playing in the dream head: 'The Blood Done
Signed My Name'. So don't let 'em fool ya:
unemployment's hard work. You gotta stay
occupied. Shadowing box, push-ups. Every-
thing is a prison of the mind, a drawer crammed
ajar with infinite unmatched ankle socks.

AMALI RODRIGO

Kintsugi

There comes a time when a lingering
brightwork is the only *tell* of love
beyond platitudes of the *radiance*

of fractures; that brokenness
is a blessing etc.
Imagine a monk's devotion

on pilgrimage, divested of all
but his robe and cup thinking only
of kneeling at an invoked chapel.

A heartland, when he enters
will find old consolations no more
or nourishing. But the chapel stands

for eternity, like a round world
that can be cupped in a palm
and filled with meat.

For now, he'll walk ley lines like cracks
on clay, the touching points
that make each fragment among another

relevant, a necessary extension.
He'll even pause at a crosswind
on a high curve and find no battle site,

no cairn where a want was set straight
on its path, but tributaries, flowing secret
and bright, that has no ocean to give

out at and no birthing spring.
I had not known how I believed
in a durable self until I saw, in mending,

a void amassing in the bowl.
What a vessel may hold, be the measure
of. How it sings.

How like a body, it sits apart
among kindred, and is safe to use.
How my arms went dead

holding it to your mouth
for your lips to open
and eat.

The Bell Is Always Ringing

All our fates are measured out as breath
– Pura Lopéz-Colome

If, to hear is a long
gathering's interruption
of this this this –
not *tongling* bronze
not the iron cast heft
of a house, not a *zhong* bell's two
exact tones, but perhaps like
someone caught
in a small act of love,
or the trace of a day he held
a hint of her at the far end
of a hallway, she, panicking
out of sight in a blur of white,
and how smug
they were of reflex
superstitions,
the anecdote pealing
through the intermittent
years until they find
themselves again, there,
in an identical corridor,
like small clappers trapped
inside a clay *ling*, diasporic
chime of an elevator
born again and again
in the muffled interior
of the hotel, rising high
or falling to the earth –
pint bell, quart bell, a hundred-
weight bell, the crystal one

with a river in it,
sundering.
How deep then the grain
in walls, anonymous doors
branded by numbers,
the affluence of light
that cannot meme a time of day –
night-watch, harvest, or wedding feast.
And spangles in lush pile,
as if only just risen
into being around the bare
toes puckering
into it.

POETS READING

> *An occasional series in which poets write about their current reading*

. . .

Frances Leviston on Lorine Niedecker's Collected Works

In his lecture on 'Lightness', Italo Calvino explains that he writes by subtracting weight from his material, and argues that lightness can be "a value rather than a defect" in literary works. His proposal seems to be a creative response to the assumptions of the word 'gravitas': its habitual equation of quality with the heavy, the earthed, the implacable; its pejorative opposition of intellectual 'light-' and 'heavy-weights'; all the problematic permutations that the metaphor burdens us with. Calvino's intervention works on behalf of those who have "[tried] to make language into a weightless element that hovers above things like a cloud or better, perhaps, the finest dust or, better still, a field of magnetic impulses".

Lorine Niedecker (1903-1970) benefits from being read in this light. The landscape in which she lived and wrote – Blackhawk Island in waterlogged lowland Wisconsin – imbues her poems with a fundamental buoyancy and instability. "Life on water," as she termed it, is a perilous, indefinite thing. Her natural poetic unit is a fleeting, irregular five or six or seven lines, a spontaneous effusion of thought or tentative linking of phenomena. Some of these effusions are left to drift in white space; most are shepherded into sequences they seem actively to resist, like flotillas perpetually on the point of dispersal. Despite this, a precarious cohesion obtains, something that withstands the buffeting of attention, and in fact seems to catch on it, and use it to travel along.

The poems' insubstantiality, which must have lain behind many a dismissal over the years, is not a failure of seriousness but a positively asserted value. It gives them a sense of being everywhere and nowhere at once; of being both warm and disembodied. Emily Dickinson is clearly a forebear in this project. Dickinson, whom Calvino cites approvingly as a spirit of lightness, seems to lie very close to the surface of a late Niedecker poem such as this one:

> Illustrated night-clock's
>   constellations
> and the booming
>   star-ticks
>
> Soon I rise
>   to give the universe
>   my flicks

The notion of the night sky as one enormous clock, each star a second's tick, is enormously appealing, and deeply Dickinsonian: I'm thinking of "A clock stopped – not the mantel's", or "It was not Death, for I stood up", which has the lines "And 'twas like Midnight, some – // When everything that ticked – has stopped – / And Space stares all around – ". But Niedecker's irreverent final gesture is not very Dickinsonian at all, and she departs even more significantly from Dickinson's example by cultivating a sense of continuity. Dickinson would have portrayed the electrifying moment at which the clocks stop ticking, but Niedecker records the ongoingness of the world. Dickinson is sudden; Niedecker is "Soon":

> Fog-thick morning –
> I see only
> where I now walk. I carry

my clarity
with me.

This sense of ongoingness contributes to the shifting, glancing qualities of the verse. One does not, in the moment, pause and grasp chronologies: "clarity" is limited. Niedecker, here in the late 1950s, is anticipating an *ars poetica* statement by one of the original Objectivists, George Oppen, in his 1968 poem 'Route': "Clarity, clarity, surely clarity is the most beautiful thing in the world, / A limited, limiting clarity."

Sometimes Niedecker's poems offer some of the same pleasures as *Robinson Crusoe*: you marvel at the hardiness and ingenuity that circumstance demands, and the will to make do, to survive. 'Homemade/ Handmade Poems' (she couldn't decide) – which was, incidentally, written years before Bishop's Crusoe declared, "Home-made, home-made! But aren't we all?" – offers instance after instance of this. A visit to the laundromat: "Casual, sudsy / social love / at the tubs // After all, ecstasy / can't be constant". There is an 'Ode to my pres-/sure pump', an indispensable item in dealing with constant flooding; and then this little poem from circa 1965:

Popcorn-can cover
screwed to the wall
over a hole
so the cold
can't mouse in

"Mouse" as a verb is clever, of course, but what really drives the poem is the "Popcorn-can cover" – a luxury item whose purchase is retroactively justified by turning the waste to good use, first as a makeshift patch, second as a poem; a cover in its original designation that goes on being a cover in the afterlife; a popcorn-can – the little popcorn-can that could. "Pop goes the weasel" is audible somewhere in the mix, as well, which is not surprising given that Niedecker's first published book, *New Goose*, drew heavily on folk rhymes. *That's the way the money goes*. We might even conceive of the popcorn kernels themselves as tiny houses into which a popping heat insinuates itself. There is something fundamentally poetic about the patch, which means the poem need not primp its language up beyond a brusque companionable practicality. Niedecker neither apologises for nor romanticises the 'poverty' of the resources from which she draws. There's no anger, no self-pity, no palpable design; but at the same time it's not neutral or affectless. There is pride here, an offhand inventory, and a sense of – a liking for – the absurdity of such measures.

The tonal palette of Niedecker's long poem 'Paean to Place', a late work of unusually sustained concentration, blends its offhandedness and homeliness with a manifestly heartfelt, fluent urgency, a summoning of all her powers. This is her *Künstlerroman*:

> I was the solitary plover
> a pencil
>   for a wing-bone
> From the secret notes
> I must tilt
>
> upon the pressure
> execute and adjust
>   In us sea-air rhythm
> 'We live by the urgent wave
> of the verse'

The poem is ecosystematic in form, composed of networks enmeshed with one another: bird-life, aquatic life, fishery, the story of her parents' relationship, her own childhood and adolescence, literary awakening, patterns of weather and flood, quotations from loved books. The light touch with which she handles all these weighty materials is astonishing, a testament to the marriage of technical skill and emotional intelligence. The poem looks like highly irregular free verse, but in fact is structured around five-lined stanzas, flooded containers, in which line plays off against stanza, syntax and section breaks, so that many shapes and processes are superimposed upon each other, and required to coexist. The poem's spatial sensitivity contributes to its highly tuned acoustic, as the shape of an environment contributes to the way sound carries through it. Niedecker is at least partly intent on replicating the soundscape of Blackhawk Island for the benefit of her deaf mother:

> I mourn her not hearing canvasbacks
> their blast-off rise

from the water
Not hearing sora
rails's sweet

spoon-tapped waterglass-
descending scale-
tear-drop-tittle
Did she giggle
as a girl?

The poem reaches only provisional conclusions: it recedes as floods recede, driven by invisible pressures and balances. Such forces are felt throughout Niedecker's poems. They are personal, but also worldly: feminist, ecological, political, without exhibiting themselves as such. And there's always more to notice – so much so that I sometimes wonder if her lines bob around, rearranging themselves, whenever the book is closed.

Lorine Niedecker, Collected Works, *ed. Jenny Penberthy (University of California Press, 2002).*

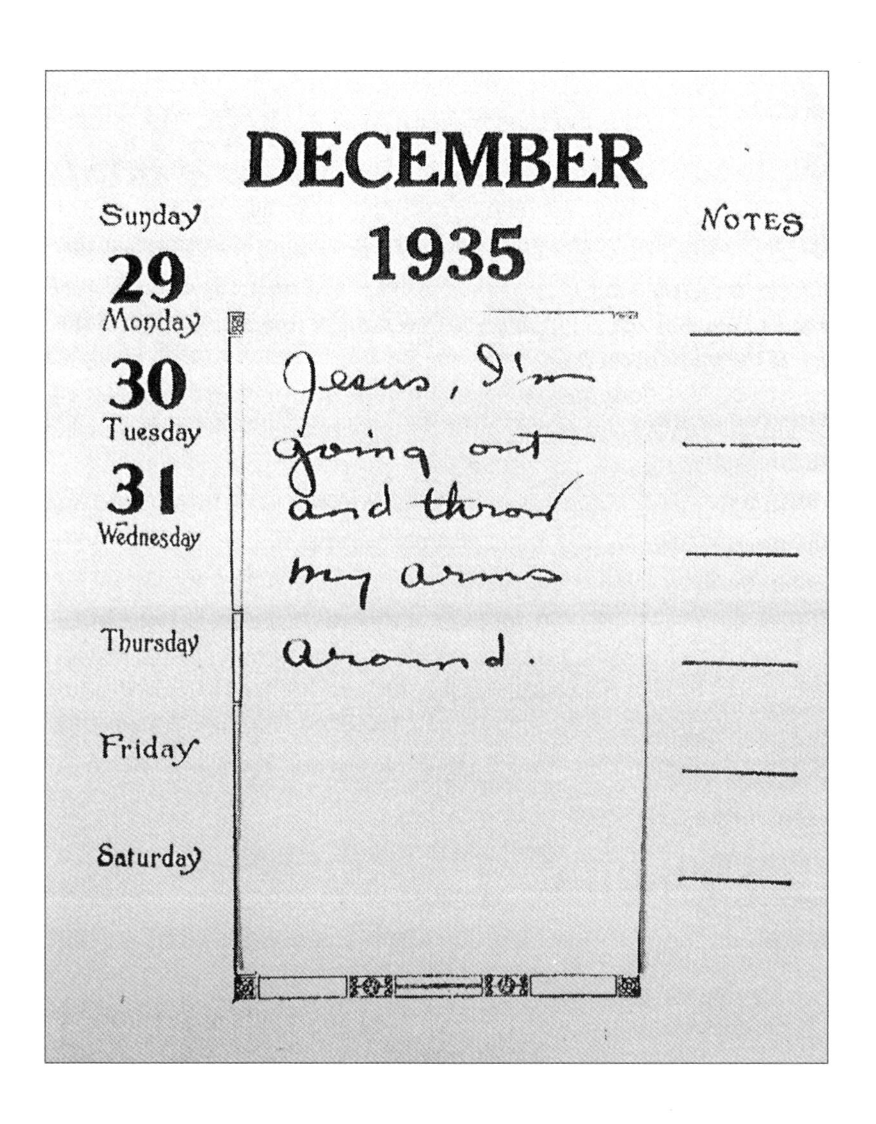

From 'Next Year Or I Fly My Rounds, Tempestuous' by Lorine Niedecker.
Image courtesy Bob Arnold, Literary Executor for the Estate of Lorine Niedecker.

Jack Underwood on Jennifer L. Knox

It was the end of the summer of 2012, the wettest for a hundred years. The Olympics were done; Pussy Riot were on trial; a woman in Zaragoza had made world news for "restoring" a priceless fresco of Christ, so that it resembled Bertie Bassett, as foreseen in the nightmares of Edvard Munch, and then Neil Armstrong died. It felt oddly like the end of an era that no one had realised they'd been living through, like Christmas was over, only Christmas was a period of Western history following the Second World War, and in the miserable January of the new era the only person who seemed to know what to do was the guy campaigning on Facebook to arrest the warlord Joseph Kony, and even he would end up burnt out by October, naked and slapping the pavement, ranting about the devil in downtown San Diego.

Back in east London I was really feeling sorry for myself. My first manuscript had sweated on an editor's desk for six months, only to be sent back with "must try harder" written in the margins, and Alt Lit had turned up like a lurid, new, sugary fruit drink we were all compelled to pretend didn't give us migraines. *How am I supposed to work in these conditions?* I asked the remaining cat, the one we hadn't found dead on our doorstep that July, the delivery man knocking, pointing down mutely. It was all getting a bit 'Skunk Hour', and while I'm not going to say something grand like "Jennifer L. Knox's poems made me fall in love with life and poetry again", it's fair to say that her first two books, *A Gringo Like Me* and *Drunk by Noon*, were the chicken soup that kept me going that winter:

> This morning Willard says there's no place else
> he'd rather be than with beautiful ladies at a pie contest.
>
> "What's yer pie?" he growls to the petite 40ish Latina
> on his right, giving her a squeeze around the waist.
>
> "A Splenda Blueberry Sweetiepie!" she says
> into the wrong camera, beaming.

('Children of the Blah Blah Blah Blah', *Drunk by Noon*)

The first Knox poem I came across online was 'I Am a Girl' about a "little bird girl with a very, / very big dick... so big it must be checked / at the airport". So far, so bird-penis, but what really struck me about the poem was how far Knox was prepared to advance the idea; behind the "big dick", a "curtain draws back: / a cave, like the innards of a geode, / the walls wink and beep tiny lights. / You can't fuck it unless you're made / of numbers." The irreverence of that kind of imagination made me feel that Anything Could Happen in her poems, which made all the other poetry I'd been reading, troubling over, measuring up to, feel dull, whiny, limited.

I knew I couldn't write irreverently imaginative poems like Knox, and that was absolutely part of their appeal; reading them felt like being twelve again: nerdily tagging along with a friend's cool big sister and watching in awe as she smokes in the kitchen in her bra, or leans through the window of a guy's car just to tell him up close to go fuck himself. Badass. Smart. Yes, Knox's poems made me feel like a little poetry chickenshit, just about allowed to vicariously get off on their sass, adventure and luxurious transgression:

> Today I turn thirteen and quit the 4-H club for good.
> I smoke way too much pot for that shit.
> Besides, Mama lost the rabbit and both legs
> from the hip down in Vegas.
> What am I supposed to do? Pretend to have a rabbit?
> Bring an empty cage to the fair and say
> *His name's REO Speedwagon and he weighs eight pounds?*
> My teacher, Mr. Ortiz says, *I'll miss you, Cassie,*
> then gives me a dime of free crank and we have sex.
> I do up the crank with Mama and her boyfriend, Rick.
> She throws me the keys to her wheelchair and says
> *Baby, go get us a chicken bucket.*
> So I go get us a chicken bucket.
>
> ('Chicken Bucket', *A Gringo Like Me*)

To me, Knox's aesthetic falls somewhere between Carson McCullers's *The Heart Is a Lonely Hunter* and John Waters's film *Pink Flamingos*. Each voice carries its own tragedy, perversion, American darkness, whether it's the family chiding their elderly father in 'Pastoral With Internet Porn' – "These nice girls just want to wash / some donkeys at $100 bucks a pop for their cheer- / leading squad so try and relax and enjoy it!"; or the speaker of 'Hot Ass Poem' telling you, whether you like it or not, "Hey check out that dog's ass wow that dog's ass is hot that dog's got a hot dog ass I want squeeze that dog's ass like a ball but a hot ball a hot ass ball."

The unsettling humour of Knox's poems is a by-product of what Gabriel Gudding describes as her "satiric empathy". The laughter her poems provokes is a kind of nervous laughter, at the "cultural horror she depicts with complicity as if she too were not entirely innocent of it" (to cite Bill Knott). Class and gender politics gnaw away in Knox's poems: tangible, but kept complex, dissolved in the kitsch and weirdness:

> Pass the meat to me, this spazz among spazzes.
> What would I be without meat? A crybaby.
> I cry when animals get hurt. I would never ever hunt anything.
> Unless it was getting dark and I was hungry.
> I'm totally freaking out.
> I could come out and say I'm totally freaking out, but this is a poem, so I will say, "Darker grows every leaf/hov'ring o'er the red, red meat."
> I'm one of those idiots who's going blinder all the time.
>
> ('59 Tenets about Meat', *Drunk by Noon*)

The role of humour in poetry is something Knox addresses in an excellent series of blogposts on funny women poets for Best American Poetry:

> The funny poet questions the sanctity of our medium's most revered trope: gravity. The graver the poem, the more important. Does the just plain stupid, irrational, ashamed, or lazy have any place in a poem? Never ever? I feel those feelings all the time... In life, no tone is constant, the line of thought always interrupted – the crucial by mundane, shame by egocentrism, peace by chaos. One moment, you're sobbing in your living room, the next, remembering there's a sale at the Gap.
>
> ('Send in the Crying on the Inside Kind of Clowns', *The Best American Poetry*, 2012)

It's also worth noting the ingenuity and precisions of Knox's image-making, as in 'The Corgis Come and Go' a high-camp lament in *Drunk by Noon*:

Now as the memory of their auburn fur
and all the ways my hand connected to it
sinks like a flaming car to the bottom
of my opaque frozen lake of feelings,
a new shape's stirring.

And there is the surprising tidiness of her writing, despite its pace and the amount of stuff she packs in. She writes the way Dean Moriarty parks cars:

I found him in the backyard at midnight
wearing a foam rubber sun costume – no tights
or underwear on – one ball hanging out the leghole
like a jawbreaker in a baby sock.
('You're F*cking Crazy', *The Mystery of the Hidden Driveway*)

In her forthcoming book, *Days of Shame and Failure*, Knox seems more pissed off and sardonically barbed. There are sadder, more personal poems about her family, like the tender 'Life's Work', but also grim, apocalyptic eco-poems such as 'The New Twilight Zone: "Empty City"', or 'Indian Head'. The poems are still funny, but life and all its waste feels tiring, hard. Which is why a poet like Knox is so necessary, and why I find her work so restorative, because poetry is rarely as convincingly defiant in the face of all our bullshit:

[...] all the people at the bar and behind the desk began to clap and cheer, and I
pivoted on my heel and marched out through the double glass doors where my
unicorn was waiting and she was like, 'How'd that feel?' and I was like, 'Amazing!'
('Ladies Night/Feelin' Right')

A Gringo Like Me *(Soft Skull Press, 2005)*; Drunk by Noon *(Bloof Books, 2007)*; The Mystery of the Hidden Driveway *(Bloof Books, 2010)*; Days of Shame and Failure *(Bloof Books) is published in September.*

Alice Oswald on Paul Stubbs's The End of the Trial of Man

For nearly two decades (or perhaps millennia) Paul Stubbs has been engaged in the task of imagining what lies beyond the imagination: "I would describe what I do to be a writing of no nation or race or even 'world', and [it] is at the very least what I would call an anti-ontological work. Thus, I could just as well do what I do sitting upon the ledge of a still-travelling comet." There is no guardrail to his kind of project, no literary guide or physical limit, only exploration.

The extraordinary thing about the poems in *The End of the Trial of Man*, his fifth collection, is that they never obey the so-called rules of creative writing. They never speak politely from the visible realm to the invisible, but, like X-rays, they get straight under the surface and make images of insides: "as along the wrought mental-wires of my brain vibrates now the voice of no God". We've grown used to a different kind of poetry. To enjoy this book you have to perform something like the backward roll of Descartes, who pointed out that the mind is much more clearly and distinctly known to us than the world. Once you've dropped the idea that poets really ought to write sensuous, sensible poems about sensuous, sensible things, then the Stubbs picture-show can start:

It was just
after the announcement,
over the tannoy,
that religion had ended,
that I felt
the overwhelming
compulsion to depart
it, heaven.
And why, still, today,
In this chair
I descend...

('The Pope Departs His Heaven')

The book-cover (the counterpart of this poem) shows Bacon's portrait of

Pope Innocent X, seated, screaming, as he descends; and it is Bacon's paintings, quietly mentioned at the beginning of each poem, that provide the grid references from which they start walking towards wilderness. Stubbs has said of the process: "The 'figures' introduced in the poems differ very markedly from the ones in the paintings, for they are not in any way part of our human activity: rather they appear transfixed by a compass which no longer directs them towards the unthinkable will of God. The poems contemplate only the world in which Bacon himself was a diversion."

Equipped with nothing: no nation, no nature, no self, no confession, no pre-established poetics and only these glimpsed flashes of Bacon's paintings, the poems make their way by voice alone. They move stutteringly along lines that wax and wane, often backsliding by a quirk of syntax that keeps throwing redundant pronouns in the path: "I felt the overwhelming compulsion to depart it, heaven"; "as if your creator had removed it your backbone like a pick". The grammar is appositional rather than sequential, as if holding its components suspended not in time but in space. The subject is post-theological, aiming (with no mercy either to atheists or priests) to "replace all of the generic icons of the world, if only for the duration of my own words, with new ones, capable of outstaring God".

Everything about the verse is transgressive and brand-new and seemingly home-made. It's no good tutting over its metrical or grammatical misbehaviour – you must just watch the visions and let the rules remake themselves. Sometimes you'll get agoraphobia from the spillage of bland words over whole separated lines ("or as if", "seems that", "when even"); sometimes you'll be zoomed through multiple couplings of language: "breath-canisters", "bone-gears", "lung-frayed", "rib-ruin". This is not the friction-tune out of which most poetry is made, in which a music is laid down and then doubled against itself so that every space represents a tension. This is not tune at all ("the idea of an aesthetically pleasing poetry is to me repulsive"), but the weird leaping-falling-stepping-style of Thought itself: "struggling to select a gait that's human".

It is reassuring (especially when hurtling through space on the ledge of a comet) to locate new poems in terms of their influences. Stubbs has been a close reader of Rimbaud and Hölderlin, both of them fierce disturbers of the forms of language. He has cited W.S. Graham as an inspiration, as well as Gregory Corso, Vallejo, Pilinszky, Gascoyne, Dante. Perhaps the boldness of his endeavour takes something from those writers, but its solidity and seriousness undoubtedly derive from Stubbs's interest in philosophy: Nietzsche, Spinoza, Heidegger and, above all, Kierkegaard. If I had to identify the peculiar, almost comical rhythm he uses, I would say it is the rhythm of Kierkegaard's Knight of Faith: "to be able to fall down in such a way that the same second it looks as if one were standing and walking, to transform the leap of life into a walk, absolutely to express the sublime in the pedestrian – that only the Knight of Faith can do".

The appeal of this book (and the loneliness and shock of it) is the authenticity of its faith – not faith in the decayed sense of something terrified and retrospective, but faith as a form of scepticism: faith staring inwards at the death of God and going on staring until something new appears beyond. There is an earnestness, almost an innocence at work in the imagery, which, in spite of its relentless pace, has none of the coldness of imagist poetry. It is warmly, biologically embodied, full of ribs and vertebrae and membranes and umbilical cords as if the body, scattered but still sensitive, were the only reliable authority: "where the human face, a tray of blood it ripples, ripples into the face of God".

It's as if, by turning his back to the earth and straining with every phrase "to arrive at a place in no-time", the poet has made himself available to all the religious and other conflicts trying to voice themselves around him:

> the construction of a prayer-machine
>   (flesh-gloves for hands
>   fixed to a bicycle wheel)
> that, on rotation, can endure at least
>   twelve separate pairs of
>   palms (at the same time
> of different faiths...).
>
> ('Religious Man Prepares for Paradise')

How do these astonishing images manage to be at once so private and so familiar? I don't know, but it's worth remembering what Tsvetaeva said about contemporary demands for contemporary poetry: "a work's contemporality... not merely doesn't reside in the content, but is sometimes there despite the content, as if jesting with it".

The End of the Trial of Man *(Arc, 2015).*

Essay

THIS HAS BEEN A BLUE/GREEN MESSAGE EXITING THE SOCIAL WORLD

Charles Whalley

Published in *Stop/Sharpening/Your/Knives 5* (2013), Harry Burke's 'in respect to the real' alludes to Allen Ginsberg's 'In Back of the Real', in which Ginsberg's speaker contemplates an "ugly" yellow flower in a "railyard in San Jose". After wondering "how can we now say / 'i wandered desolate'", as Ginsberg's speaker did, Burke's poem ends:

> i sent bella a message
> (she is the flower of the world)
> of a rose
> which i decided to colour yellow
> not the yellow of ducklings
> or bellies
> or our great eastern future
> but my own
> r 255
> g 255
> b 0
> yellow

RGB values represent how colours are displayed on screen by mixing red, green and blue. The intensity of each constituent primary colour is specified by a number between 0 and 255, and so here the speaker's "own" colour is the maximum of red and green: the brightest, simplest yellow. Whereas the dirtiness, the worldliness, of Ginsberg's "flower of industry" allows our reading to convert it into symbol, Burke's speaker attempts to refuse complications of his message. The interruption of the RGB numbers in the final lines, with "yellow" withheld until the end, marks the distance that this perfect, digital colour puts between conventional poetic manoeuvres and Burke's rose, using computer language to say what other words can't. It has exchanged its old limits for new ones. Expressed in RGB, the yellow can't be any brighter.

Ginsberg's poem, itself playing among Wordsworth's daffodils, feels like a Romantic consciousness doing a warm-up exercise, or attempting it with the dirtied materials in view. Burke's, on the other hand, asks whether it's necessary to be lonely, or rather to aestheticise the experience of loneliness and solitary contemplation in an age of connectivity. Instead of the fiction of soliloquy, the event of Burke's poem is the act of communication with which it ends: the message "of a rose" sent to "bella". '[I]n respect to the real' shows how our relationships with others, and how our cultivation of our selves, are dependent on the methods we have to exercise them. It demonstrates how lyric subjectivity is a product of its socio-economic context, and how it negotiates for space with the technologies that enable it.

When the influence of the internet on poetry appears in anthologies or in surveys of contemporary writing, it is generally shown to have produced writing that fetishises the web's strangeness and novelty – poetry that is alive with excitement at the new possibilities offered by networked computing at the start of the new millennium. The two strands typically presented are Flarf and conceptualism, with writers such as Drew Gardner, Sharon Mesmer and K. Silem Mohammad in the former camp, and Kenneth Goldsmith and Vanessa Place in the latter. These writers produce work that is collected and collaged from online sources, as statements about the internet's vast, exhilarating, unreadable excess of the boring and the profane. Flarfists create kitschy, outrageous, burlesque poems from the results of Google searches. Nada Gordon's 'Unicorn Believers Don't Declare Fatwas', for instance, begins:

> Oddly enough, there is a
> 'Unicorn Pleasure Ring' in existence.
> Research reveals that Hitler lifted
> the infamous swastika from a unicorn
> emerging from a colorful rainbow.

Conceptualists, somewhat similarly, elevate the technical mechanisms of the digital circulation of words – typing, copying, printing – into conceptual elements of composition, exploring the nature of language as material. Noah Eli Gordon's *Inbox* (2006), for instance, is a book-length poem created from the body of every email in his inbox, in one unbroken paragraph. For both Flarf and conceptualism, cyberspace provides fodder for a detached, curatorial poet to process and collage, as if in thrall to this new reading experience. And encouraged by the formerly nerdy nature of the internet and the outsider status consciously sought by these poets, this writing is generally compartmentalised into specialised and unthreatening peripheral categories, such as 'cyberpoetry' or 'digital poetics'. The internet's presence is reduced to an extension of twentieth-century avant-garde practice, as a set of compositional strategies, in a cursory acknowledgement of the information age as a matter for the squabbling children of L=A=N=G=U=A=G=E poetics.

Poetry's dot-com bubble – these conceptualist provocateurs and Flarf hooligans – was a response to the conditions at the new millennium, a techno-utopian vision of the thrilling brave new world online. But the economic and technological structures of the internet have undergone significant change since Y2K. Much of this comes under the developments behind 'web 2.0', whereby technologies such as Ajax (introduced in 2004) allow a website to become more like a dynamic application than a static document, encouraging user participation and interaction, updating effectively in real time. These developments encouraged the increasingly social web that we recognise today: Facebook was launched in 2004, YouTube in 2005, Twitter and Tumblr in 2006, and so on. Facebook is now the second most visited website (after Google), with more than a billion users. Social media are now more popular than porn. What's more, the first iPhone appeared in 2007, moving smartphones beyond the business market and into the hands of more than a quarter of the world's population by the present day. By 2010, internet use in the developed world had more than trebled in a decade, and the internet had changed from being something one dialled from a computer in a study to something always-on and in the pocket. As the cloud replaces the superhighway, the internet has become something that passes over us rather than something we surf over, something intervening throughout our work and social lives, something that attempts to know us better than we know ourselves. And so as the boundary between off- and online disappears and as the internet flattens into reality, the novelty, fear and excitement fade. The distinction between the author and the internet disintegrates, as the internet becomes no longer the source of waste material for a detached poet to process, but a collaborator in the active, endless work of self-creation and expression. It is no longer a separate place to go for information, but the medium in which we are ourselves.

In visual art, the term 'post-internet', albeit with some modishness, has been used to describe the work arising from this context, as contemporary artists acknowledge the ubiquity of the internet in all aspects of artistic creation and circulation. Marisa Olson, credited with coining the term, describes it neatly in terms of the artist's everyday life: after going on the internet, she makes art. More specifically, Gene McHugh defines 'post-internet' in relation to the shift described above:

> The Internet, of course, was not over. That's wasn't the point. Rather, let's say this: what we mean when we say 'Internet' changed and 'post Internet' served as shorthand for this change.
>
> So, what changed? What about what we mean when we say 'Internet' changed so drastically that we can speak of 'post Internet' with a straight face?
>
> On some general level, the rise of social networking and the professionalisation of web design reduced the technical nature of network computing, shifting the Internet from a specialised world for nerds and the technologically-minded, to a mainstream world for nerds, the technologically-minded and grandmas and sports fans and business people and painters and everyone else. Here comes everybody.
>
> Furthermore, any hope for the Internet to make things easier, *to reduce the anxiety of my existence*, was simply over – it failed – and it

> was just another thing to deal with. What we mean when we say 'Internet' became not a thing in the world to escape into, but rather *the world one sought escape from...* sigh... It became the place where business was conducted, and bills were paid. It became the place where people tracked you down.

In the past few years I've been exploring (see http://postinternet poetry.tumblr.com) how this context and outlook are also reflected in contemporary poets, especially those who, if born around or since the late 80s, have likely not known a world without the internet: writers such as Gabby Bess, Steve Roggenbuck, Melissa Broder, Tao Lin, Patricia Lockwood, Mira Gonzalez, Harry Burke, Sophie Collins, Crispin Best and Sam Riviere, among others. These writers produce innovative, exciting work that is profoundly influenced by living on or with the internet in the 2010s, as a period when the conditions of a poem, or for a poem, have changed.

An example to start would be Crispin Best's 'if you don't forward this poem to 10 people i will crawl out of your toilet while you sleep and i'm gonna be pretty ticked off', published in the 2014 anthology *I Love Roses When They're Past Their Best*, edited by Harry Burke. Best's poem starts with the speaker and another "playing the intel jingle" on a piano, joyfully quoting a marketer's tune. The second half of the poem then runs:

> we stop
> i pet your head and say
> "we stopped"
> and
> "that's ok"
> and
> "girl you put the baller in ballerina"
>
> i feel like
> do leaf insects know other leaf insects aren't just leaves
> and
> it's late

A nervous love poem, the speaker appears to keep talking to defer an overwhelming question. The present-tense space sets up frames for its own statements, as the poem exists in an uncertain position between the action it relates and the jokes it is able to generate from them. The speaker delivers his lines while winking at the audience, always sort of putting on a voice, even if it's his own. As this moves from direct to something like indirect speech, the rhetorical question about "leaf insects", discarded as quickly as it is introduced, is given as something the speaker 'feels like', as if its relation to the drama of the poem is in its emotional meaning, as if the line is a self-contained poem.

In part, the hyperactiveness of this poetry derives from the internet's attention economy, but it also reflects the changed relationships between speaker, voice and poem in post-internet poetry. With the web 2.0 technologies described above, the internet presents a flattening of the distance between consumption and production, between composition and publication, forming a closed loop with the potential for almost immediate feedback. Poets accustomed to working within a textual vernacular produce poems that are acutely aware of their medium, that seem to work within a continuous, immediate, ongoing present, a sort of self-enclosed, self-directed free indirect discourse, where the speaker anticipates, repeats and frames their utterances. These poems are continually looking for space for more text within or without their current frame. They are always self-consciously 'quoting'. Instead of stable voices, whose emotion recollected in tranquillity has been processed and ordered to emphasise epiphanic resolution, insight and memory, these poets present speakers actively in process and acutely aware of their own textual self-construction.

In this tendency, Best perhaps sits most closely to the poets grouped in and around the label 'Alt Lit' – primarily young American writers for whom writing is an extension of, or even indistinguishable from, their social media presence. (Tao Lin and Mira Gonzalez have a book of "Selected Tweets" forthcoming this year.) Steve Roggenbuck, perhaps better known for his YouTube videos, is a central figure; he recently co-edited an anthology of Alt Lit-related writers, *The YOLO Pages*. He has 17,000 followers on Twitter. Roggenbuck's 2013 ebook of "poems and selfies", *IF U DONT LOVE THE MOON YOUR AN ASS HOLE*, includes lines such as the following:

> im pissed off "band of horses" is not actual horses.
> what will it take to get some god damned actual
> horse's into the studio because i am willing to

Illustration by Austin Cowdall.

> do what it takes. i want to have a gigantic bird
> mask on my face everywhere i go. WHAT WOULD
> U SAY if u knew it was your last comunication
> with anyone, for ever? my favorite moment from
> the office is when michael scott quits and tells
> david wallace *You have no idea how high i can*
> *fly*. The World Series of Christianity. a person at
> this party recognized me from the internet, they
> seemed upset that i exist IRL. im not totaly sure
> how to "double dog dare" but im hangin out
> with 2 dogs right now im thinkin of goin for it

A previous set of poems, *DOWNLOAD HELVETICA FOR FREE.COM*, was entirely created from Roggenbuck's own instant messaging logs, as if sourcing Flarf from himself. In the above, he is producing it directly, with an irrepressible chattiness that feels potentially endless, veering from near sarcastic to earnest. But unlike Flarf, it makes no distinction between internet and poet, between source and curator: rather than going off to the internet for material, the writing comes from the internet in the first instance. And while Flarf's compositional process allows the poet to disown and exploit its kitschy silliness to amuse or offend, Roggenbuck instead uses indeterminate irony to achieve something similar, with droll exaggeration allowing him to not (quite) take responsibility for his words.

Just as the serial work of social media trains us to interpret messages in reference to their sender, the central drama of post-internet poetry is that of disclosure, confession and self-creation. A crucial development of the internet since 2000, concurrent to the rise of social media, is a decline in anonymity, one of the reasons for excitement and nervousness with the early internet. (A popular cartoon in *The New Yorker* from 1993 had the caption "On the Internet, nobody knows you're a dog.") Marketing companies (and post-9/11 governments) have a keen interest in our lives as data, in our activities, circumstances and consumer preferences. Facebook incentivises disclosure so that we may be better sold. But any relief and reassurance in being known, of having our identities reaching out across networks, brings the new anxiety of maintaining an authentic, original, irreducible self in the face of machines that anticipate our self-creation. One strategy of eluding this is with the mischievous, playful irony as utilised by Best and Roggenbuck, an interpretative shield to protect the poem from a single reading traceable to the author. But another is in more impersonal methods of expression, eschewing or at least complicating direct speech from a lyric 'I'.

A useful, and final, example here are Sophie Collins's unsettling centos in *I Love Roses When They're Past Their Best*, from which the anthology gets its title. 'kissing' runs:

> I remember the neck curls (limp and damp as tendrils)
> symbols, and secret names
> before I knew there were men
> or improvised concoctions with tequila
>
> ridiculous and lovely,
> I weigh you now against the good you've done

It was composed by searching title words on the Poetry Archive website and taking one line from each of the results. But unlike Flarf or conceptualism, it doesn't foreground the compositional process by re-contextualising non-poetic language. By taking words from other poems, 'kissing' is not all that different from a traditional cento, or from Collins's own writing. In an interview, she mentions how producing them felt like "the process of simply writing a poem", and goes on to liken the centos to stories that we come to confuse with our memories, that we incorporate into our own personal narratives. As the work of the speaker switches between what the lines say and how they are collected, depending on how we think of the poem, it isn't ever entirely clear who's speaking. We remember that our words are always somebody else's. By making the number of results the determinant of length, the centos are statements of the limits of the Poetry Archive's inclusions, but also of the print canon beyond it, as the internet comes between the poem and its tradition. Further, the internet becomes an element of our reading, as, when we go about the business of interpretation, we begin to incorporate the functioning of the Poetry Archive's search algorithm in our idea of the author as delimiter of meaning. The technology and its operation here determine the boundaries of how we read, as rather than being a subject or main element in a process, the internet is a ubiquitous filter, medium, container, intercessor.

In poetry, as in everyday life, we are continually working through and negotiating with technology, with what it allows us to do and what sorts of people it allows us to be. Writing itself is a technology. These recent changes in the reception and composition of literature, changes that continue apace, remind us that our aesthetic concepts in poetry arise from the context in which it is produced. Post-internet poetry, like the internet itself, anticipates the abolition of its own specialisation, and so ultimately of its own usefulness as a label. When we reflect upon the influence of the internet on poetry, we must do so within the fundamental questions of literature: what effect does this technology have on how I think of myself, on how I express my identity through language, on how I communicate with others? We can't talk about poetry without now also talking about the internet.

Charles Whalley is a poet and freelance critic.

PHILIP GROSS

Storm Surge

It isn't the children
down here at the sea wall
in the dim and storm-stretched
late dawn, the light
discomposed by the wind,

but the grey,
the middle-aged and more-than,
though the children we were, or
didn't dare to be, then,
are here with us, too –

in that grin
between neighbours who other days
could pass for strangers, that glee
in our hop, skip and stumbling
back from the edge

when it breaks, a muck-
brown ruckus, wave-slosh
going nowhere but suddenly
here, at large amongst us,
on the prom, a golem

still unsteady and out of its element
but, hey,
it could like this life... then
crash –
crumpling back, so we're left, touched,

brushed against,
a little breathless (the radio
warned us; that's what brought us
running), half proud
of this wet sock, that slap

on the face,
the quite surprising weight of it,
the great tidings it brings... still
with me now, hours on,
its mute melee and heft

in my closed eyes,
how a twenty-mile-wide swell
comes unpicking the seam of itself
down the slant of the sea wall,
how it gathers up

its skirts and leans
into a head-down hunching run
as if a mad Rococo ball turned
rugby scrimmage; one makes a break
down the touchline

to that final thud in the crook of the pier,
our *yes!*
as if this was a kind of victory
for us, too. To be
here. So very here. So very small.

Coming to Slow

for Wyn Mason, at 50

Slow arrives, more suddenly
than quick can. Here is where Slow lives,
between shutter and click,
tick and tock. In no time. Say it's *relative*;
I see the old, the dim-doddery
one in the family the others don't get round
to visiting. You do. Flinch
a little when Slow, now, takes you by the hand

and leads you outside, to the shock
of night air, to space and its clockwork, stars
that seem stopped in their tracks,
coils of glittering wire – the way a river wears
its bracelets, whips a steady
spinning top of eddy or exfoliates its never-
ending scales of light. Study
this, and what is quick, what slow, and where

are we? One moonless night
I tried to slow my pulse and breath to test
the speed of it, not the light
but the seeing, on the fifty-mile arm-stretch
of darkness that was Severn Sea.
Could I be still enough to count the flicker-blips,
their different frequencies, each me-
me sign among the masthead sparks of ships:

light-buoy, warning beacon, red,
white, green? Their telling pauses, a prickle of risk
on lethal waters, likewise a code
of comfort, silent morse whose slow-slow-quick

I couldn't hold, that human eyes
can't grasp: past, future in a present tense of flow
our language lacks. *Sub specie*
aeternitatis... We try. The first steps are slow.

Small Songs of Carbon

Those oval nubs of rubbers
in (those days) every school-
boy's pencil case – sweets
sucked by the beast of carbon,
its black spit.

•

Up in the higher Hs
every pencil is a lethal weapon.
Sharpen it with care.
Sloppy Bs,
on the other hand (mucky fingers)
just don't see the point;
they are almost a fluid,
good for shading, moulded shapes,
not outlines, nearer, further... where
we live, in tender blur.

•

The fine-as-grey-snow sift
from riddling the grate –
one puff
and it stands in the air
beside you. Moves when you move.
Won't lie down again.

•

The moment when the sweep's brush cocked
its implausible snook from the chimney –
like a secret, out,
                    what every family in the street
shared: soot.

•

His fingers, black
with charcoal: who wouldn't want that,
to be drawing with remembered fire?

No signature, a thumbprint
on the paper. On his wife's cheek. What

you work with long enough, you
particle by particle
become.

•

Fire counts
in minutes – carbon,
centuries.

•

Oh, and what can you say about diamond –
the same stuff as us, as life, but
          gone to heaven, so
emptied of itself, all weakness, so
                    inhabited by light.

If you didn't love it, you would say it hurts.

NICK LAIRD

Rescue Remedy

Maybe Schwarzenegger's an acceptable exploration of the Nazis
and the red embroidered velvet book is chained up in the nave,
but human skin contains so many receptors for gentle pressure,

deep pressure, sustained pressure, follicle bending and vibration,
that maybe all our edges will get rounded down and no one ignorant
of geometry ever re-enter. Maybe these Nevada palominos at a gallop

hundreds-strong draw the same subsiding trail of dust across the desert
as when the Christians took back Spain or Dylan went electric.
Maybe the fourth magus was just a bit busy, and maybe you do say it

like you're only saying lightning is corrective of an electrical imbalance.
Maybe it was Pliny, when he held a naked flame against an amber bead
and smelt the tang of pine and realised it was resin, and not a teardrop

wept by Neptune. Maybe some species can be successfully domesticated
and some just can't. Deer, for instance, have proved remarkably resistant.
Perhaps the giant vomited the moon up only after great pain in his stomach.

. . .

I could say thank you, say it's not the three-metre moustache or a slow day
in London town's second-best opium lounge. It's blue, say, or maybe
red or green, maybe strange, bottom, charm, down, top, up or antiup,

anticharm, minus-blue, minus-green, minus-red. Maybe the moonlet,
my little cloudlet, dog encircling me all morning maybe, watching.
Perhaps a golden plover with its two-note song is the prime glossator

of our time and what matter the neutrinos pass through does not
specifically exclude you. If there does exist a history to study
of the strictly curtailed – Dunwich, for example, Tunguska, Chernobyl –

the lizard also spat the sun back out again, and maybe the majority
of Hopi chose the desert so they'd never have to not pray for rain.
Maybe metaphor works backwards, too. Star of Bethlehem for shock

and mustard seed for the deep gloom occasioned by no earthly reason.
Say the desperate Romans prayed at the Temple of the Last Resort. Say
pine for guilt, hornbeam for exhaustion, chestnut for mental congestion.

. . .

Or Joshua demanding the sun stand still, though notice how in *Terminator*
he just
keeps coming. Maybe I would like to say a word or two about that nothingness,
if I may. Inexplicably, one must be heavy like a working engine, but not a rock.

Maybe death is implicit in the ticking of the metronome but the real gift of
fish oil, particularly cod, is that it has been proven to reduce the symptoms
of osteoarthritis and boost your brain power. Say, maybe it is all invisible

from space, yes, but also say you noticed in the grace of Duncan Edwards
the anonymity of style true to both his kind and his kind of generation.
I only say what the headlines say – *History Is Less Than 48 Hours Away.*

Say drought it was, and thirst, and aqueducts that first gifted us the arch.
Say Byzantium was nothing but expansionist slavers and ingenious trash.
Say the vaulted roof of Wells Cathedral leaves me as impressively empty.

Say, we really should call someone. Say the warlord I stayed with in Split
had the given name of Dragon, and a perfectly serviceable coffee table made
from four upstanding shell casings and a square pane of tempered glass.

. . .

Say the laws of physics favoured the emergence of our consciousness
and maybe I would like to say a word or two about *Kindergarten Cop*,
or maybe not. Agrimony for mental torture behind a cheerful face.

My father says the only time he ever saw his own father cry was after
the Munich air disaster. Say of Pangu, when he died, how his voice
became the thunder, his flesh became the earth, his hair the trees,

his sweat the rain, his bones the rocks and mountains, and finally
the men were left as little armoured insects to crawl across his body.
Say the working parts operate at such a pitch they cease to make a noise.

Say they keep on glimpsing the doe and her fawn at the edge of the clearing
at dawn, and for thousands of years. Lawrence argues to the very end
it's not so much cricket that's a metaphor for life but the other way round

and impossible not to note still this immeasurable but hyper-real force
your body works upon my body's mass – even at this distance and after
all the days how much I want this, all of my hands paraphrasing your skin.

The Good Son

i

The deconstructionist in us might gloss
that last request as *Bring back my phallus.*

I'm thinking how even after Hamlet senior
stage-whispers *Adieu!* to his son, his heir –
his piglet and little poppet, his lovely –
how he begs him again *Remember me,*

since he can't help himself, and the actor
says it back and swears it on his honour,
and by convention is meant there and then
to whip out his sword and avenge, avenge –

but sits down instead, shrugs off his mantle
to undo his satchel and pulls out a quill
and a clean pad to get it in detail –

which the Elizabethans deem a scandal.

ii

We did. We paid upfront but understood
that all accounts would soon be met
and every tab discharged in full.

Each loss incurred a debt
and hard to get the registers to balance.

This side of Cookstown Gospel Hall attests
in giant gothic font –
For the Wages of Sin is Death...

then a few yards round the corner,
nailed up in Monrush to a telephone pole,
an unfaded statement in fairly crude
red, white and blue on plywood –

Murder in Texas gets the electric chair.
In Magherafelt you get chair of the council.

iii

The rigor functioning in Sophocles
as justice we cannot retrofit with peace:
an animal language inadequate
to state the state of the state.

Hard to think some companies
were simply unafraid to leave
aside the long soliloquy:

natural, simple, affecting

Garrick had the whole fifth act rewritten
so when Claudius orders Hamlet
to get *immediate* to England, his reaction
is to draw his blade, and let him have it.

I mean that Hamlet stabs him.

GERALDINE CLARKSON

Love Cow

Oh cow of love you have me pinned
to your evergreen felt

and are in at my ear with fermenting
oaths and actual importuning

and imprecations. I rebut you
with a tough raft of arguments, derived

from magazines under the sofa
at my Aunt Libbie's house

I have a disease, your rump is small,
your rich cream disgusts me

and others which are more
sophisticated, from the Bible and books of

philosophy. You give me a soft brown
stare. How I wobble now before you, cow

of love, humongous, like a free-range
sack of boulders swaying

delightfully, your cordial spine
rippling, your celtic skeleton

offering promise. To eat you
would be divine, surely,

your emerald milk fast-forwarding
to your stomachs, pressed over and over

by clenching muscles. Why is it you cows get
such bad press? I wonder, half-beguiled.

Sometimes I see you, fenced,
defending young ('let go of your dog

if cows surround you', the notice
on the farm-gate says)

or at the abattoir, steaming hot
and hung prosaically on hooks.

Or on the plate with no relief
except for some mocking green

salad – staked out, defenceless.
They say your flesh can stay

unsullied in the gut
for six months or more –

bowels fill with longing
for sloping fields, a faraway sea.

Dora Incites the Sea-scribbler to Lament

Sees him at the far end of the strand,
squamous in rubbery weed, his knees bobbing
urchins, his lean trunk leaning, sea-treasure for her.

After it all (they mate, like carapaces, in parentheses)
Dora feels coolness in new places, lifts a reused
razor shell, mother-of-pearly and straight

and signals out to the swell of mouldering green.
Dora is electric, in love, and deep water.
Dora, Dora, Dora, in which dread is.

People people the beach, peering
through splayed hands, appealing:
DAW-RAAaargh. A boat sees her passing.

Sea-scribbler's chest buckles
in after-shock:
his quill is primed: squid-inked and witful.

GREGORY LEADBETTER

Stalking

Between the fingers of the falling dew
I find a path that takes me through
the sleeping eye to where it wakes
on the other side of the dream it makes

I tread the moss that beds the hoof
I follow into absent proof
a moth without a moon
a wanderer with the day's wound

my fingers are lichen and as slow
my mirror the yew that blisters the shadow

the gift I bring for the darkling birth
is stillness suckled from my breath

I spring the roe and the world in hiding.
The branches grip. The horned are watching.

Imp

On the bad days, I shooed her mews away
out of nothing but an absence of joy.
I never installed a back-door flap for her,
so she would patter all night to get in at the window
while I lay wide-eyed and sleepless, pretending not to hear.

I know it was a blessing
when she landed like a fly on my forehead
as I was trying to write,
her cicada rustle scribbling in and out
before the flick of my hand sent her to hide
in the plumbing, where she whined for weeks
until I found her, toad-shy and morning-blind
in the kitchen sink. I held her, for the first time then,
revived her with what has become her favourite wine.

It has often been her game
to go missing. It is where she thrives,
as if she delights in being imagined –
looked-for in the fading light,
or at the beck of a buzzard's call.
In the garden, I would find her spraint,
stinking of rotten fruit and putrid grain,
the tang of iron and the fume of honeycomb.
She would announce her return with a black-out
bite through electrical cable, then creep in close, dab
my eye with a spider-leg to see if I was awake.

She could drive me mad
with her cuckoo blink –
then I remember how she would
pull me out of the O of a dream

when I couldn't breathe
and make me a day-bed from her sloughed skin.
She would lap at whatever saltwater
leaked from me. It wasn't right
for her to see me cry,
but she would tongue my tears away,
curl me a rabbit-fur snake
for a pillow and blow through my ears.
Her opalescent gaze could break
the world-egg open
over and over again.

Tonight, I will leave out a bowl
of blood and marrow to tempt her back,
fall asleep on the sofa, wait
for a child's hand to touch my face.

LAURA SCOTT

If I could write like Tolstoy

you'd see a man
dying in a field with a flagstaff still in his hands.

I'd take you close until you saw the grass
blowing around his head, and his eyes

looking up at the white sky. I'd show you
a pale-faced Tsar on a horse under a tree,

breath from its nostrils, creases in gloved fingers
pulling at the reins, perhaps hoof marks in the mud

as he jumps the ditch at the end of the field.
I'd show you men walking down a road,

one of them shouting to the others to get off it.
You'd hear the ice crack as they slipped down the bank

to join him, bringing their horses with them. You'd feel
the blood coming out of the back of someone's head

warm for a moment, before it touched the snow.
I'd show you a dead man come back to life.

Then I'd make you wait – for pages and pages –
before you saw him go to his window

and look at how the moon turns half a row
of trees silver, leaves the other half black.

The Half-loved

Sometimes you hear her, breathing heavily,
climbing the stairs to find you in the room
where the old silk wallpaper still clings
to the walls. And then you feel her sighs

tightening around your ribs as she rehearses
her lines one more time so she can tell you
exactly where you went wrong in a voice that cuts
through your chest. Sometimes you see her

swaying in the doorway, churning the ground
under her feet like Hannibal's last elephant,
tired of all that armour cutting into the folds of her skin.
Sometimes you taste her in the dregs of your wine,

swirling in the bottom of your glass and then,
she cuts you off, mid-swallow, until your throat
remembers all those conversations you turned
with a skier's grace when they got to the precipice

where the love should have been. The half-loved
remembers everything – every slight you ever dealt her,
every letter you sent her. Sometimes she runs
her fingers over the white space around your name

until the paper is as soft as cloth, and pictures you
putting down your pen and thinking of someone
else. The half-loved saw it all, blinked it in
through her dark lashes, and is weeping it out today.

CAROLINE BIRD

The Fear

Every day I picture you dead.
Splayed between two traffic cones,
unresponsive. Punched into prayer
beneath a windscreen's cracked sky.
Face down in a puddle of yourself.
If you're two minutes late, I sense
police on the porch,
                their loaded lips.

We are the laughing lovers
in the reconstruction, just
moments before the attack.
The happy times. Pre-crash.

Last night, in bed, your arms
hurt like a jolted seatbelt.

The Amnesty

I surrender my weapons:
Catapult Tears, Rain-cloud Hat,
Lip Zip, Brittle Coat, Taut Teeth
in guarded rows. Pluck this plate
of armour from my ear, drop
it in the Amnesty Bin,
watch my sadness land among
the dark shapes of memory.

Unarmed, now see me saunter
past Ticking Baggage, Loaded
Questions, Gangs of Doubt; my love
equips me. I swear, ever
since your cheeky face span round
I trust this whole bloody world.

IAN McDONOUGH

Lupins

I came to understand that lupins
had made me their human avatar –
their representative among the sentient,
an ambassador in the walking world.

I spoke eloquently to all who'd listen
of how lupins, cultivated and wild,
stood as flags, signposts,
lanterns, signifiers, masts –
were, in fact, nature's cursors,
printing, indicating, highlighting
aspects of that great, green book
we walk among, between, within.

When I have served my time among the humans
the lupins will admit me
to their ubiquitous but hidden land
where, rich with perfumes
and slow botanic truths,
I will come into my flowering.

Perturbation

A stranger came to the village,
spent a handful of days
at the Harbour Inn.

When he spoke you listened,
but afterwards
lost most of what he'd said.

Nor, in his absence, could we picture
his hair, his mouth,
the colour of his skin.

When he left the seagulls wept,
and Miss George, high
in her tower, sang

of apricots and desert blooms,
of moistnesses
and serpents' eggs.

F.J. WILLIAMS

The Sleep Council

I admire those who can sleep on armchairs
leaving a small ruin of themselves behind,
a squashed cushion, the shape of the head,
a single earring slipped down the sofa:
it's never enough just to drop off.

And there are those who prefer a blanket
to the soft ambush of the furniture,
elbows in, knees up to the chest, curling
their weakest spots into the fabric, leg, belt
and groin while the party dies around them.

Some sleep with the plough and hunters in the sky.
Others find grace in awkwardness, discomfort,
disappearing on a mountain, pitons
stuck for ever and a sling of chain.
Some wait within the ice until the spring.

There's the one-pound-bed in the lodging house,
lost razor, toothbrush and billy-can,
and the hot-bed shared in shifts;
the hammock on a ship slackening overnight,
the plank-bed that returns us to the sea.

In the east, sleep means a casket,
loft arrangements, making yourself a yurt,
the *frazz* of antiquity like a lilo,
a bag for meditation you fill with breath
that serves you during zazan at the dawn.

I think of the heart, three parts fire, a scan.
I'm holding out for fragments,
the power nap, forty winks, a doze
in the leadened, dead exactitude of schedule planning,
waking up with items clanking in the brain's tin cup.

How easy to miss a life and disappear
beneath a snowfall of emails, sales receipts,
in the failed state of work, endure crap sleep
and have black eyes and sit this one out.
Now we have a list, the Sleep Council tips

for spikes in anxiety and Aphrodite's bed.
Click to find a showroom on the web;
a flameproof mattress to *remember* your shape.
Now twilight gives an hour for pillow talk.
And brings us tales of immortal men.

STEPHEN PAYNE

Translating the Proverb

The Japanese say
Not seeing is a flower.
But don't look away

from whatever scene
draws your gaze. Don't close your eyes.
That's not what they mean.

Not quite. The saying's
point is that it's possible
to overthink things.

Some propositions
can't be proved: the better truths
are intuition's.

And if I've somehow
always known this, still I learned
it again just now,

escaping the glare
of information to breathe
some chilly March air,

when it came to me
where the path to the field turns
past the cherry tree.

SULIS AND KIM

Frances Leviston, Disinformation, *Picador, £9.99*
ISBN 9781447271147
Sam Riviere, Kim Kardashian's Marriage, *Faber, £10.99*
ISBN 9780571321438

reviewed by Tiffany Atkinson

...

The 'keenly anticipated collection' is a publicity cliché, but few books are more keenly anticipated than second volumes from poets whose debuts received especially high acclaim. This is true both of Sam Riviere, whose *81 Austerities* (2012) won the Forward Prize for Best First Collection, and of Frances Leviston, whose *Public Dream* (2007) was shortlisted for the T.S. Eliot Prize, the Forward Prize for Best First Collection and the Jerwood-Aldeburgh First Collection Prize. Readers who enjoyed these will find that each poet's distinctive and different idiom is deepened in the new work, even while, as poets of the same generation, they apparently grapple with a shared 'contemporary moment'.

In spelling out this contemporary moment, the cover blurbs of both books bring to mind a second critical commonplace, one that makes a virtue in itself of deconstructive attitudes towards subjectivity, knowledge and language, as though this weren't now a default setting, or rather – especially for poets trained in academic discourse – a common departure point rather than the sum of a finished work. Thus *Disinformation* wonders "How we [have] come to know what we think we know", while *Kim Kardashian's Marriage* "is as refractive as it is reflective, and disturbs the slant on biography until we are left with a pixellation of the first person". But the more interesting point is perhaps not so much how the poets take things apart, but how differently they both desire and manage to wrest significance from this predicament.

In this respect, Leviston's poetry is the more conventional, if by conventional we mean unafraid to place the linguistic marker of the speaker/thinker throughout the poems as a reasonably consistent point of mediation, an 'I' that invites the reader *into* the thought process rather than slipping distractingly out of reach – together with a cumulative concentration so intense it reads almost as an act of linguistic will. Leviston, like Elizabeth Bishop, whose influence is acknowledged directly in the poem 'Bishop in Louisiana', is brilliant – almost claustrophobically so – at the precise unfolding of a probing consciousness on the page. Often the stanzas are so intricately constructed that it is difficult to excerpt a section without doing the overall effect an injustice. For example, here is the opening of 'The Paperweight':

> From Chambord-pink at the base, it clears
> to where the upper curve reflects
> a skull-cap of charcoal, giving the Earth's atmosphere
> in miniature: the sea, the air, then space.
> Erupting from that wavy cocktail is a white flower
> like a frozen whale-spout arrested mid-expulsion,
> a filigree fuchsia trumpet, petals
> peeling in a spray [...]

Disinformation establishes its steady gaze through a tripartite structure that moves outwards from local domestic disturbances – "Like a wet dream this snow-globe was a gift / to myself... Mantelpiece matryoshka, / she wears an inscrutable face"; the IUD that "plants a dull pea under the mattress", or the paperweight made thick with significance over six stanzas of acute detail. The middle section more expansively reaches for the traces of a golden age [in which] "we communed with gods. / A god could be hidden, barely contained, / inside the costumes of normal men". At a literal level, a sequence of 'curtal' sonnets brings the Celtic goddess Sulis back from comparative obscurity; more figuratively, Leviston's poetry tunnels beneath the surface of situations to explore their innermost workings in a way that creates an almost pagan suture between world and consciousness: indeed, the world often serves as a metaphor for the workings of the mind – "[the clouds'] long shadows / outrace us underfoot like thoughts"; the gate of Propylaea is "a huge tautology // made of marble"; "mud-crusts offer up / proof of a mind that quickly wove / its ringed design"; "water like wisdom resists capture". These images seem almost at odds with the collection's title, or rather the collection overall seems confident in its ability to probe beneath the tackiness of the surface to find something more integrated and enduring. This unflustered intelligence is at its most controlled in the final section, a series of studies in Leviston's trademark concentration that frequently make a gentle imaginative leap between the observed and the mythologised in a way that seems effortlessly sage, making it surprising that Leviston is so young. Here is the opening stanza of 'Caribou':

> With muzzles made blue
> by the blue saxifrage they cultivate a weakness for,
> their heart-shaped chests, their little bibs
> and dewlaps fringed with long white hairs like radish roots,
> they show how thin our myths for them are.

What this style perhaps sacrifices in terms of swerve and surprise is more than made up for by the concentration and range of the poet's gaze, and a brainy recursiveness that deepens rather than dazzles.

Kim Kardashian's Marriage, by contrast, is dazzlingly recursive in a way that works the surface/depth relationship as a kind of trompe l'oeil, like the facial contouring make-up – primer, highlight, etc – that gives the book's sections their titles. While Leviston seeks depth and resonance in even the most resistant places, Riviere peels the linguistic skin of internet culture away from anything that might ever have been construed as sincere. Thus the epigraph, Kardashian's plaint, "*I want that forever love*", floats like a discarded plastic champagne flute on the surface of the poems. As with *81 Austerities*, the collection's material is harvested from search engines and curated by way of collage and improvisation; unlike *81 Austerities*'s ostensible themes of social justice and exclusion, the 'field' of this book is the 'furore' (really?) of Kardashian's famously brief first marriage, and more generally the fetishes and paraphernalia of contemporary celebrity and 'lifestyle'.

Pushing the torsion of self-referentiality even further, and as though language itself were a natural resource in short supply, the titles of the poems are all recycled from the meme-y section titles of *81 Austerities*, so that the already oblique 'Girlfriend Heaven', 'American Hardcore', 'Spooky Dust', and so on, become 'infinity hardcore', 'girlfriend weather', 'grave pool'... The effect of the titles alone, over ninety-six pages, is like looking at a reflection thrown back and forth between mirrors, holographic and infinitely relayed. The poems themselves are deft exercises in irony, non sequitur and clever line-breaks, and are often weird and surprising:

> I'm starting a band
> about the negative fan reaction
>
> to November.
> Over half are women aged 25-44.

Or,

> I really surprised myself
> with several patios and intricate corridors,
> antiques saved from around the world

and,

> Since I am a model I have to think a lot
>
> inspiring picture
>
> for my security and protection
>
> we heart it

Apart from the epigraph, it is unclear where, if at all, the text originates from Kardashian herself: the point, perhaps, is that there is a kind of slick, jaunty impersonality to the harvested text that makes identifying a particular 'voice' a frankly silly and outmoded idea. This is presumably also true of the 'improvisation' element, where Riviere himself has contributed a hinge between fragments of found text. The name of the *actual celebrity* (almost an oxymoron – all celebrities are virtual) in the title works like a sort of fetish, promising a revelation or intimacy that never, of course, arrives. Kardashian, if anyone was hoping for poems *about* her, like all cultish goddesses is always elsewhere. The book is as clever as it is provocative, and borderline exhausting, as experiments pushed to their limits often are, and if it weren't for *81 Austerities* I'd say it was a one-off. The effect is almost relentlessly ironic, yet there is something still residually 'confessional' about these bytes of text, arguably made more plaintive by their bewildered lack of context (what, for example, is the story behind the stilted English of a phrase such as, "Trust you to confuse whether she virgin or not"), and their crafting into elegant Faber-ish stanzas and surreally beautiful images such as "Much of its relaxing greenery / comes in a little glass vial". It is as if the many-headed desire-machine of the internet had somehow forced itself into press while the poet looked on, amused and maybe a little anxious. Of course, we know better: this style is now inimitably Riviere's, an originality without traceable origins, which is the paradox of the undertaking. And once a poet has tested the limits of impersonal modes of composition, where does he go next? In the case of both poets, we may indeed find ourselves keenly anticipating.

Tiffany Atkinson's So Many Moving Parts *(2014) is published by Bloodaxe.*

THE VIRTUAL AND THE PHYSICAL

Sean O'Brien, The Beautiful Librarians, *Picador, £9.99*
ISBN 9781447287513
Frank Ormsby, Goat's Milk: New & Selected Poems, *Bloodaxe, £12*
ISBN 9781780371252

reviewed by Harry Clifton

...

Sean O'Brien belongs to, and has to some extent mentored, a group of poets including Don Paterson, Ian Duhig, Paul Farley and Michael Donaghy that emerged in the 80s and early 90s at a tragic time for the Old Left in Britain, when its mining communities in particular fell victim to savage rationalisations, a late and perhaps final form of the ideology we live under to this day. He has a wistful poem, 'Another Country', in his new collection about the loyalties and betrayals of that period:

> Scattered comrades, now remember: someone stole the staffroom tin
> Where we collected for the miners, for the strike they couldn't win,
>
> Someone stole a tenner, tops, and then went smirkingly away.
> Whoever did it, we have wished you thirsty evil to this day:

> You stand for everything there was to loathe about the South –
> The avarice, the snobbery, the ever-sneering mouth [...]
>
> The North? Another country. No one you knew ever went.

The past, like the "North", is another country. Its principal feature, if I correctly read the epigraph "Get there if you can" by W.H. Auden, is moral inaccessibility. You can get there by train – there are many train journeys in O'Brien's poems – but if you tried to disembark, you would instantly brain yourself against an ideational screen, and realise that the things you see are Platonic essences, the people are not people but types, and the landscape itself a kind of *paysage moralisé*, not real in any physical sense but a field of moral speculation. Sometimes, as in the Orwellian 'Thirteen O'Clocks', it is a landscape out of Auden's 'The Shield of Achilles':

> A yawning execution squad
> Is mustered in the still-dark yard,
> Unshaven and unbreakfasted
> And for a moment hard to know
> Apart from the condemned,
> Who enter by another door.

At other times, as in 'The Lost of England', the Philip Larkin of 'The Whitsun Weddings' is omnipresent:

> The journey too conspired to evade: somewhere at hand
> Lay cities we would never visit, and instead we seemed
> To slow continually inside the rainy summer heat
>
> Through nowhere much, that might have been the Midlands
> And might not, past nameless settlements and cooling towers,
> Chains of ponds, canals where nothing moved [...]

Larkin, in fact, that supposed arch-Conservative, has been crucial to this group of supposedly Left-leaning poets, not only as an instructor in modern stanzaic form, but for his shock juxtaposings of demotic and aureate. 'Dialogue in the Multi-Function Room' is one of many instances in O'Brien:

> Let us turn grotesque disparities
> Between distinct symbolic orders to
> Rhetorical advantage. Tear his effing head off.

I expected, having read some of the more virtual scenarios here, to find in the title poem librarians out of Borges presiding over infinitely extended Babels of information. Instead of which (it is no criticism), the "beautiful librarians" are a rewrite of Larkin's old racehorses in 'At Grass', gently eliding themselves from a virtualised society and taking what is left of the physical world with them:

> Never to even brush in passing
> Yet nonetheless keep faith with them,
> The ice-queens in their realms of gold –
> It passes time that passes anyway.
> Book after book I kept my word
> Elsewhere, long after they were gone
> And all the brilliant stock was sold.

If Larkin and Auden, both moralists, like O'Brien himself, cast long shadows in the virtual landscape, it is Wallace Stevens who drives the train. The priorities are not William Carlos Williams's "No ideas but in things" so much as "No things but in ideas". Everything here is ideational, semi-abstract, and you will like or not like these poems according to your preference for the physical or the moral. Not that there aren't exceptions, as in the charming 'Do You Like Dickens?' with its flesh-and-blood boy and girl caught up in a holiday romance in real-time Youghal:

> You were a poor boy, a paperback, suitable
> Only for poolside amusement. What did she call it?
> The common pursuit: but she read you from cover to cover.

But they are exceptions that prove the rule, which, like it or not, is the loom-and-shuttle interweaving of abstractions out of late Stevens. Subconsciously, from the diminuendo of hearing-loss at the start to the placeless room at the end, *The Beautiful Librarians* is an elegy for the lost particularity of the senses. "The greatest tragedy", as Stevens writes in 'Esthétique du Mal', "is not to live in a physical world". The staffroom tin in 'Another Country', besides being part of the miners' tragedy, is part of an even greater tragedy of its own.

If one group of "boy-actors", in Seamus Heaney's phrase, was assembling itself in Britain, another had long since come together in Northern Ireland, around a different moment in history. One of their elders, James Simmons, in the early 80s published a poem beginning with these lines:

> I hear that Ormsby will be leaving soon,
> That only leaves me Longley and Muldoon.

In fact, it was Muldoon who left, while Longley (who introduces this *New & Selected Poems*) and Frank Ormsby kept the flame alight in Troubles-torn Belfast. Poetry being as it is, a tortoise-and-hare business, it has taken this long to bring together a coherent retrospective of one of the most quietly respected voices of that region, less visible than some of his more glamorous peers, but just as likely to last:

> When McQuade went up for a ball
> he came down with snow on his heels,
> and when McQuade took a shot the goalie
> had to hitch-hike back to the field:
> a legend from the tall decades behind,
> like 'Bawler' Donnelly and the Night of the Big Wind.
>
> A quiet cancer stopped him, its tackle sly,
> decisive. Shocked I watched him fall
> saw death collect him, easily as a loose ball.
>
> ('McQuade')

Economy and wit are the dissecting instruments, and an ear, a terrible lightness of touch, as impeccable as R.S. Thomas or Bernard O'Donoghue. Nothing overstays its welcome, and that can be said of Ormsby as a whole, whose four collections average one every ten years. In many ways, and read alongside the intellectually agile if textually abstract world of Sean O'Brien, he belongs to the pre-technological, pre-professional era of poetry, where livings were made separately from 'being a poet', and where word and thing, hand, eye and spirit had a different, almost neural interrelatedness – a world in which, again to paraphrase Heaney, we still believe what we see, hear, touch.

If O'Brien country is and is not England, Ormsby country is always somewhere you can find on the map – physical, grounded, dimensional, expressing itself through its own particulars. Here a soldier stationed near Lough Neagh waits for the invasion of Europe:

> The bigger fish have country cousins here.
> At their own depth soneghan and gillaroo
> dart in the quiet loughs and are not found elsewhere.
>
> I dry on the shore and imagine the world renewed
> cleanly between two islands I cannot name:
> as a rounded stone, say, that the ebb left bare,
> or light on water the morning after a war.
>
> ('Soldier Bathing')

And here, more domestically, a set of common objects are ranged against a darkness that could be history, virtuality, sheer oblivion:

> a paintbrush steeped in turpentine, its hairs
>
> softening for use; rat-poison in a jar;
> bent spoons for prising lids; a spare fire-bar;
>
> the shaft of a broom; a tyre; assorted nails;
> a store of candles for when the light fails.
>
> ('Under the Stairs')

I emphasise the physicality of his work because Ormsby's, strictly speaking, is a post-religious world that still, nevertheless, believes in what Stevens calls "the folklore of the senses" and Keats called "primitive sense". The very thing O'Brien struggles with is what underpins Ormsby.

In a body of work extending from Fermanagh through Belfast and taking in an American sojourn, a synthesising myth, be it Christian, Classical or esoteric, might have been part of the agenda. But Ormsby, unlike his Belfast coevals, is not a mythmaker. Each separate poem, wherever it is set, is there to make sense of the dimensional world. Let God and the heavens take care of themselves. Human ashes belong in the hour-glass of temporality:

> If I must be 'the remains', let me be so
> as a soft grain to your living.
> You can look to me daily for an hour
> of silent company,
> or tell at a glance you're running late again.
> ('The Hour Glass')

Modesty, selflessness, yet no loss of intensity. Many a hare, or seminar-room favourite, will find itself overtaken by this particular tortoise.

> *Harry Clifton's* The Holding Centre: Selected Poems 1974-2004 *is published by Bloodaxe.*

CARROT AND STICK

Michael Hofmann, Where Have You Been? Selected Essays, *Faber, £30*
ISBN 9780571323661

reviewed by John McAuliffe

...

Michael Hofmann is both a tremendous enthusiast for the poets he loves and a vengeful prosecutor of those he feels have sold the art short. His new book of essays is a brilliantly written tour of the Hofmann horizon. More substantial than *Between the Lines* (2001), his previous collection of mostly short pieces, it retains that book's characteristically idiosyncratic rhythms and sharply sweet-and-sour tones. Even a reader who disagrees with Hofmann will savour the way he frames his arguments for and against his subjects: poets and poetry, translations (and translated), the lives of artists.

Over the decade in which the essays accumulated, Hofmann's translation (and editorial) work has accelerated rapidly. There is an accordingly large if not quite comprehensive section of the new book devoted to that side of his work: passionate advocacy in the case of Gottfried Benn and other esteemed German-language writers and artists, as opposed to, say, the fiction of Stefan Zweig, which gets the full Hofmann treatment. Look away now, those of you who enjoyed Wes Anderson's adaptation of Zweig in *The Grand Budapest Hotel*. For Hofmann, Zweig is "sodden, formulaic, thin, swollen, platitudinous". Such vituperation is sporadic. He is consistently down-at-mouth about 'developments' in poetry: "Poetry in America has declined to a civil war, a banal derby between two awful teams, and in Britain to a variety show (albeit, I suppose, a royal variety show)", which nods to recent laureates as well as, beautifully, to "royal" as a kind of sweary intensifier. One favoured contemporary is "a carnivore if not a cannibal in the blandly vegan compound of contemporary poetry". Benn is the opposite of "state poets", who are "useful, obedient and subsidised".

Hofmann's passions are usually communicated in great rushes of adjectives and adverbs. Conscious of his own weakness for the adjective as judgement, he defends it as if he invented it. Or as if his favourite writer, Robert Lowell, had. Writing on Lowell (repeatedly, again), he declares that Lowell made the adjective "respectable", itself an odd choice of adjective (he attributes to Adam Zagajewski a similarly salvific feat with the adverb). In a typical, self-reflexively adjective-heavy paragraph, he argues: "An adjective, an adequate adjective, is a thought or a perception. Where – as often happens in Lowell – adjectives come in twos or threes, they are constellations, distinctive and collusive, radiant with outward meaning and human prediction, and held together by inscrutable inward gravitational bonds."

If his adjectival style has become more intense and assured over the past decade, it occasionally feels mannered when he pans a writer. Eviscerating Zweig, Grass or Zbigniew Herbert's most recent translator, it can sometimes feel that Hofmann is playing a part, that he has become a great one for doing someone. When writing about Elizabeth Bishop, a poet he clearly admires but whose overwhelming popularity he finds off-putting, he wonders what it might be like to pan her. It comes easily: she is, he almost argues, "sybilline", "immaculate" and, eventually, a "dystopian Beatrix Potter".

However, like most of his British contemporaries, he is strongly drawn to the fractures of the American mid-century that he reads through Bishop's writing: he is brilliant on Lowell and Bishop's correspondence, interesting and biographical on Weldon Kees, pickier about Berryman, whose strange English second life no one, surely, could have predicted; and it will be no surprise that the one contemporary American poet he discusses is Frederick Seidel. Lowell, then, continues to preside as Hofmann's modern poet par excellence: he is the yardstick used to measure all others. Seidel is credited with "an incredibly highly developed ability to 'do' his teacher, Robert Lowell". Reading Ted Hughes, the references feel more bolted on: would anyone other than Hofmann say, of Hughes's poem 'Remembering Teheran', that one line is a "a little like Lowell", another features a "Lowellian pairing", while a third line "is Lowell"? It is as unconvincing as it is enjoyable.

But, aside from his usefulness as a sort of north pole for Hofmann's critical compass, does Hofmann have anything to say about Lowell? There is, for instance, nothing here about Lowell's relationship to his progenitors Auden and Yeats, whose quarrels and transnational poetries prefigure Hofmann's interests in Lowell (and whose testy modernist-to-postmodernist relationship seems to shadow his understanding of Bishop's relationship to Lowell). Instead, the ins and outs of his defence of Lowell are narrowly conducted via his reading of Bishop, although there is a glancing, backhanded acknowledgement, in his celebration of James Schuyler, of John Ashbery and Frank O'Hara's "reflex opposition" and "distaste" for Lowell. (How celebratory is Hofmann's Schuyler essay? "I had," he writes, "the (for me) heretical thought that perhaps I liked it [Schuyler's poetry] even better than Lowell.")

In the UK, Hofmann is unexpectedly sympathetic ("the greatest English poet since Shakespeare") and brilliant on Ted Hughes. There are speculative pieces on modernist outliers Basil Bunting and W.S. Graham (whose disdain for "plastic Scots" he seconds). A single slight piece on Seamus Heaney this time, instead of the larger place Northern Irish poetry (Heaney, Muldoon, Paulin) previously occupied in his critical imagination. Here, he reads closely a three-line poem, '1.1.87', without noticing – until, he tells us, a student pointed it out to him – that the poem is a haiku, apparently missing the additional clue to its formal nature in the poem's title. It's strange too that Hofmann, so interested in patrimony in his own poems, is so disgengaged here from Heaney's late-developing reimagination of sons and fathers, a turn which might be said to begin with this poem.

The book is packed with terrific close readings, which often feel as if Hofmann is humming along with the poems he discovers for us, dwelling on each word until its particular resonances for the poem under discussion become apparent to all. (Is Hofmann's workshop the place where New Criticism went?) With some of the poems discussed here, or Ian Hamilton's poetics of subtraction, it is hard to know how anyone can supplement his exhaustively perceptive, play-by-play, 'as-live' reading of them. And he has, as anyone who reads his poems knows, a terrific ear. His Anglo-American experience also makes him expert on the import-export of British and American English: "Lowell rhymes," he tells us, "with vowel or towel"; Ian Hamilton's "bloated" demands "the careful British dental *t*, not the drawled American half *d*." And he has a translator's love for the untranslatable, loving Bunting's "writing English like a foreign language", a skill with which he also credits Pound and, of course, Lowell, whose 'Dunbarton' ("I lanced it in the fauve ooze for newts") is one example of his writing a "wild interstitial English entirely his own".

It may be on linguistic grounds, his relish for idioms and new sounds, that Hofmann approves a couple of colonials. Les Murray is a poet whose appetite for the world he marvels at, and then uses as an example by which he can find other poets wanting. (Every idea in the book is both a carrot and a stick.) While a reader will be glad he made the effort to salute Murray, his discussions of Australian poetry (and Karen Solie) seem amazed, really, that poetry happens at all in places like Canada and Australia. The workaday biographies of the Australian poets he lists in a review of one anthology persuade him to coin an embarrassing new compound: "ethnosociobiographical". On Solie, whose work he praises, there is something arch about his declaration: "how tremendous that all this exists". But then how many books of criticism do you finish by wishing for more?

The news in this book is not that Michael Hofmann remains obsessed by Robert Lowell; it is not, either, that try as he might to discover new eminences (and it would be interesting to read him not just on Seidel and Murray and Solie but on other originals, Anne Carson, say, or Louise Glück, or Kathleen Jamie), he is dismayed by the absence of a central poet in the English-language world. The news is that, in every essay here, he is still writing critical prose so enjoyable and engaging that it fits Bishop's description of the work of *G.M.* Hopkins (as Hofmann names him): "not a thought, but a mind thinking".

John McAuliffe's new collection, The Way In, *is published by Gallery.*

GIRL POWER AND ALCHEMY

Rebecca Perry, Beauty/Beauty, *Bloodaxe, £9.95*
ISBN 9781780371450
Sean Borodale, Human Work, *Cape, £10*
ISBN 9780224099844

reviewed by Kate Bingham

. . .

Rebecca Perry was sixteen going on seventeen the year 'girl power' first entered the *Oxford English Dictionary* as "a self-reliant attitude among girls and young women manifested in ambition, assertiveness, and individualism". The Spice Girls were over and tweenies who'd grown up chanting "I wanna, I wanna, I wanna, I wanna, I wanna really, really, really wanna zigazig ah" had music of their own to come of age to, but like it or not, what it was to be a British girl had changed profoundly. There had always been *types*, but now, liberated by some new level of irony, girls could alternate between Ginger, Sporty, Scary, Posh and Baby as they wished. One of the defining qualities of Perry's debut, *Beauty/Beauty*, is precisely this freedom.

The collection is divided into seven parts of six poems each. Part II, 'MY SKIN IS', takes the theme of love. Part IV, 'WHEN A DOG GOES TO HEAVEN THE STARS ARE GREEN', is mostly to do with pets. Other sections – like these, named with excerpts from the poems themselves –

are less obviously curated. Perry loves titles, and seems to relish the disjunctions of mode and register between them. Part I's yearning 'THE HUMAN HEART IS CURVED LIKE A ROAD' abuts the manifesto opener 'Pow', whose title conjures Roy Lichtenstein's thrown punch, while the poem itself is a warning to readers:

> Though I am listing flowers   I am not thinking of flowers.

'A Woman's Bones Are Purely Ornamental', at the very end of the book, likewise advises not to take its girlishness too literally, remembering of school:

> We learnt tricks
> like how to make our collarbones
> as prominent as possible
> and how to be interested
> without being too interesting.

The poems in *Beauty/Beauty* are full of enjoyable, vivacious repartee like this, their arguments unwinding through gentle syllogism, repeated words, returning phrases, and witty non sequitur. Their presiding narrator – Perry herself perhaps – an authentic-feeling hub of inner conflict, is sentimental and cynical, and often, in 'Kintsugi' for instance, both together:

> I would apologise,
> but love is the soft parts of us.
>
> [...]
>
> The feeling of remembered love
> is so easy to put in the oven and heat up.

As the slash in the title suggests, *Beauty/Beauty* is interested in plurality. Perry's role models are not pop stars (though the shared surname did make me wonder if that final poem referred to the more famous Katy's hit 'I Kissed a Girl'), but Lady Jane Grey and the Old Norse shieldmaiden Hervor instead. In a collection otherwise without name-checks, the little mermaid and Lilya from Lukas Moodysson's 2002 drama *Lilya 4 Ever* also make an appearance. What connects these four female beings? Something to do with fathers perhaps?

Perry displays a plurality of poem-models, too. There are eight 'white' poems here that feel organic and entirely confident in form. They vary, but all have the same instant visual pull, drawing attention to individual words and clusters of words as part of the shape of the whole (much as Cornelia Parker's suspended explosions invite the close-up look), and the same almost hypnotic emotional pulse. By bringing what Glyn Maxwell has described as the silence of white into the body of these poems, Perry is able to articulate uncertainty and enact the pause between finding one right word and the next. With its wide-spaced margins and concentrated mid-line text, 'Sweetheart, come' creates its own tempo, surging and slowing with barely controlled excitement. Sparsely populated 'Over/wintering' runs down the page like rain on a window. 'Other Clouds' is a pillar of strength on the left of the page, but fritters and shreds to the right in a visual echo of its subject, the narrator's stepping away from her father.

Richly self-reliant, these are poems for the girl-power generation. In a world where all is relative, subjective and ironic, their breakages and weaknesses and contradictions get as close to something like sincerity as most young poets dare.

. . .

The follow-up to Sean Borodale's *Bee Journal* is a journal of cooking whose poems, says the blurb, "were written 'live' among pots and pans". If you live among pots and pans already, this may not seem an exciting prospect. Borodale sees the kitchen as "the alchemical heart of home... a stage for acts of eating and uttering". Lucky him.

Superficially, this book has a modest feel: there is no contents list, and the poems are headed, not named, by recipe, ingredients, or instruction. Seasonally presented and tasting "of homestead phenomena, the forest-road's lay-by" ('Damson Ice-Cream'), the food is slow, artisanal and often wild. Sometimes, when bread, cheese or beer are on the menu, it's literally alive. The poems are wild and alive, too: their grammar is restless, their language essential and wide-ranging. Violence animates Borodale's raw ingredients, in 'Garden Salad' for instance, where the leaves "are dying, really dying / in the water washing them". Even processes acquire personality and intent: in 'Testing the Set-Point of Jam', "A heaviness wanders through the pan" denotes cooling; in 'Radicchio and Bacon with Linguine', frying becomes "the unfailing disturbed hiss / of sorting wetness from dryness". Borodale has taken to heart Frost's famous teaching: "Like a piece of ice on a hot stove the poem must ride on its own melting"; the poems in this collection seem to thrive on a sense of their own recklessness.

Of course, *Human Work* isn't only about cooking. Mankind may have come a long way in the two centuries between Brillat-Savarin's aphorism "Tell me what you eat, and I will tell you what you are" and today's less-nuanced well-being mantra "you are what you eat", but some things never change. As Kathleen Jamie writes, more explicitly, observing a pathologist at work on pieces of colon in her 2012 essay collection *Sightlines*, "we are predators and omnivores, we are meat and made of food". Our human work, in other words, is transformation: the transformation of dead into living flesh. Beginning and ending with apples – "apple that once was *the* apple" ('Curd Using Windfalls') – Borodale explores this idea across a wide philosophical/mythological landscape in which the poet's task is to skin, reduce, pulp and sieve "a language".

Ignoring the genealogy of recipes – their commonly maternal line – the poems quote instead from ancient Greece and allude to prehistoric hungers. The kitchen is a cave "painted darkly" ('Kipper') or

> [...] the hut of our time, it spans generations:
> in smoke walls,
> a fume's roof canvas pitched
> over stewing beefstock.
>
> ('Oxtail Stew')

Cain and Abel, St Sebastian, Gawain, Grimm and Solzhenitsyn are evoked, but the only non-mythological woman in this world is an unnamed seventeenth-century witch. The blurb, again, says *Human Work* is "the narrative of a voice in domesticity". But, in 'Curd Using Windfalls', emphatically not domesticity as most understand it:

> old times hang about my work;
> tasks in pre-mother tongue, of chores still resonant.

There is a place here for softness, too, in the brief and tender 'Blackcurrant Leaves Steeped in Cream' and 'Old Bread for Bread Pudding (To Prepare)', for instance, and Borodale has a lovely talent for writing about children. But even in a poem as innocent-sounding as 'Toast and Honey', Aesop's – and Arnold's – sweetness and light becomes something darker:

> This is the toast:
> honey pours through its holes;
>
> I let dogs through a forest.

And that darkness dominates the collection, literally: the word is used in a third of the poems, sometimes more than once. Cooking (especially in winter) is often nocturnal, so darkness – the black glass in which Borodale polishes his own reflection in the marvellous Hughes-scented 'Washing-Up' – is perhaps its natural habitat. But even in 'Roast Beef (At Noon)' it is the "half-livid reverence: / bright-eyed, dark-mouthed" of meat-eaters that this poet sees. Violent and ancient, cookery is reclaimed in *Human Work* as one of the dark arts, and in spite of Borodale's vigorous, delicate, thoughtful relishing of a universal subject more universally important now than ever, part of me still wants to tut like a housewife and mutter this is what happens when you let a man in the kitchen.

Kate Bingham's third collection, Infragreen, *is published by Seren.*

LOYAL TO THE QUOTIDIAN

Alice Fulton, Barely Composed, *W.W. Norton, $25.95*
ISBN 9780393244885
Claudia Rankine, Citizen: An American Lyric, *Penguin, £9.99*
ISBN 9780141981772
Jane Hirshfield, The Beauty, *Bloodaxe, £9.95*
ISBN 9781780372464

reviewed by Aime Williams

...

The claustrophobia of grief is everywhere in Alice Fulton's *Barely Composed* – from the "escape chamber" of the prefatory poem to "the guts of a house" where a mother lies crying. Collections often carry blurbs declaring the poet's concern with loss and death – but this book – whose subject is a mother's death and the ensuing chaotic emotions – seems more courageously about those things than most. Despite, or perhaps because of the underlying emotional charge, the poems are often highly wrought and textured: "styling something blobbish and macabre / into something pointed, neat".

This wroughtness is not just aesthetic: the book questions the extent to which composure can be 'bare'. Is it possible to be too composed, so lost in composition that expression dissolves in the anxiety of hiding the truth from oneself? 'Triptych for a Topological Heart' is a neat example of Fulton's virtues and vices in this sense – the messy heart is 'composed' neatly into a triptych, but the cloying rhymes indicate over-composure, a trapped-ness.

In this vein, though, Fulton is master of pushing her poems to the limits of the sugary sweet, playing around with the boundary between sarcasm, sentiment, and the self-harm of deliberately mis-articulating emotion. 'Triptych', which is gently rhyming throughout, ends: "Even when I'm in the dark I'm in the dark with you." The tone is so wonderfully inscrutable; it's not quite sarcasm, not quite naivety. Sometimes she slips up playing this trick:

> And if anyone says what the hell
>
> are you wearing in Esperanto
> – *Kion diable vi portas?* –
>
> tell them anguish
> is the universal language

This is a shift too far into the whimsical, followed by a thud too hard into hyperbole. But it is a rare error.

Fulton's preoccupation with unspeakable or foreign languages manifests itself in unusual ways: the book is invested in exploring the lies we tell ourselves and others to survive, and the languages that we lie in. 'Forcible Touching' features a grief-counsellor sanguinely advising against allowing children to develop fantasies following bereavement. This is set against the backdrop of a Philomena narrative, and a tale in which someone with broken English seems to be torturing animals.

Extreme psychological states are cast as a kind of destructive loyalty to the dead; various 'revelators' appear to caution against too much remembering. God never appears, although Christian imagery sometimes shows up in a surreal and unstable way, as in 'Doha Melt-down Elegy':

> I've heard that from darkness
> the mind can gestate halos
>
> made of interred glow. I've heard she dissolved
> into those rays and those rays dissolved

into the body of my mind, my brain.
But you won't find her anywhere

unless you put her there yourself, the revelator said.

Unhelpful memory is a preoccupation of Claudia Rankine. In her fifth collection, injustices build up to an intolerable level. As well as poetry, the book contains photographs, essays and scripts. Some of these seem more purposeful than others – a picture of Danish tennis player Caroline Wozniacki posing as Serena Williams by stuffing towels down her top and shorts is startling ("Racist? CNN wants to know if this is the proper response"). Rankine's mini-essay on Williams, documenting injustices suffered on the tennis court – unfair calls, unpleasantness and harassment from journalists and colleagues – is one of the most helpfully upsetting segments of the book.

The collection is compelling and the experience of reading it is exhausting. This seems the point – it's exhausting to read, much like the repeated instances of minor racism (the "quotidian struggles") are to its subjects. These range from unnamed, seemingly middle-class women to high-profile cases of teens shot dead by police. They span the Atlantic, just about – from Jordan Davis, an American teenager killed in 2012 by a man who objected to his rap music, to Mark Duggan, shot by a police officer in Tottenham.

It's in the piece dedicated to Duggan that Rankine most explicitly explores one way in which racism is left unchallenged, sometimes by those who mean well. The narrator, characterised as "a middle-aged artist", is faced with a fellow writer "with the face of the English sky" who obliquely refuses to write about Duggan. "How difficult is it for one body to feel the injustice wheeled at another?" she asks. "Are the tensions, the recognitions, the disappointments, and the failures that exploded in the riots too foreign?"

What the book makes clear is that the preoccupation of a white person not to appropriate the experience or suffering of another – often a well-intentioned, politically motivated will to listen and understand – can itself morph into a reassertion of 'the other'. To not write about Duggan because you are white, Rankine implies, is tantamount to saying that because he is black and you are not, his death is not your problem to write about. Moreover, she points out, she and her fellow writer perhaps have more in common with each other than either of them have with Duggan: "With your eyes wide open you consider what this man and you, two middle-aged artists, in a house worth more than a million pounds, share with Duggan."

In light of this, it's interesting that so much of the book is about anger, and whether or not someone has a right to it. Expressing anger is so often a taboo, but what if it is actually just an appropriate response to oppression that too many people don't notice? Rankine's own anger is quiet, resolute: "The world is wrong. You can't put the past behind you. It's buried in you, it's turned your flesh into its own cupboard. Not everything remembered is useful but it all comes from." Against this, a white YouTube star encourages aspiring artists to cultivate "an angry black nigger exterior", and "wryly suggests black people's anger is marketable", says the narrator. This, when juxtaposed with Serena Williams's plight – where the "angry black woman" trope is levelled at her again and again – is troubling.

Jane Hirshfield's *The Beauty* also has a loyalty to the quotidian, but of an altogether different sort. The book is full of poems that manage to combine a series of recognisable styles – often the sparse, cryptic statement is played off against the everyday. The poems are usually sparse, each having been formally fragmented to some extent, though curious little vignettes rub shoulders with longer, carefully rhythmic lyrics.

Although her poems usually make their statements simply and without fuss ("without memory / or judgement"), the line's yearning for attention is occasionally too visible. One of the greatest successes of this mode of writing is the well-timed profound statement. However, failing to attain that profundity, and looking either embarrassingly try-hard, or a bit mad, are dangers.

Hirshfield does play around with the idea of such failure. 'A Photograph of a Face Half Lit, Half in Darkness' is comprised of a series of possibly profound, possibly not-that-profound images:

> A train station where one train is stopped
> and another passes behind it,
> heard, but not seen.

But this image runs alongside sentiments that seem to be asking the reader to think, although the nuggets offered sound a little like they might have been stolen from a self-help book: "We live our lives in one place / and look in every moment into another." I'm not sure what this poem is doing: is it a probing question mark placed over the low standard set for what passes as profound these days, or is it a poem missing its target?

Hirshfield also writes sustained poems, but she still sometimes lives dangerously on the edge of conferring significance too heavy-handedly:

> I stopped. I ran. Wanted closer in every direction.
> Each bell stroke released without memory
> or judgment, unviolent, untender. Uncaring.
> And yet: existent. Something trembling.
> I – who have not known bombardment –
> have never heard so naked a claim
> of the dead on the living, to know them.
>
> ('All Souls')

The tripling is a little much, the colon and emphasis on "existent" too operatic. Although there are a few instances of this throughout the book, when she pulls off the trick, it does work. 'Two Linen Handkerchiefs', a two-line poem, uses the power of the quotidian to gesture effectively towards the large and abstract. Like a haiku, it needs its title read in the same breath:

> **Two Linen Handkerchiefs**
>
> How can you have been dead twelve years
> and these still

Sometimes the poem seems a little too like James Wright's 'Lying in a Hammock at William Duffy's Farm', except the build-up to the final line – the distraction from mortality – is written in a curious combination of aphorism and L=A=N=G=U=A=G=E poet-esque play, with a spareness that is Hirshfield at her best:

> Long ago, someone
> told me: avoid or
>
> It troubles the mind
> as a held-out piece of meat disturbs a dog.

Aime Williams co-edits Oxford Poetry *and reviews for* The Spectator *and* TLS.

SMELL THE OIL AND TASTE THE FEAR

Sujata Bhatt, Poppies in Translation, *Carcanet, £9.99*
ISBN 9781847770202
Selima Hill, Jutland, *Bloodaxe, £9.95*
ISBN 9781780371498
Blake Morrison, Shingle Street, *Chatto, £10*
ISBN 9780701188771

reviewed by Judy Brown

. . .

Sujata Bhatt's *Poppies in Translation* keeps busy, chiming one language against another, mapping place onto place. Its flowers, birds and butterflies (especially the poppies) sometimes serve to measure or mark these shifts. This lengthy collection is a deceptively comfortable travelling companion, its light but exacting touch balancing tragedy and sweetness.

The title is open about its linguistic preoccupations and there are delicate moments where the poems negotiate with silence, or reveal how using words changes us – and them ('A German Education'). The book overflows with transformation, verbal and otherwise. Birds imitate baby calls ('Another Muse') and a language unshared with neighbours loses its symbolic quality to become "a festival of fruits, and a festival of birds" ('Truth is Mute').

Of course, the poppies flower in a number of languages (and colours):

in the words of Ingeborg Bachmann and Paul Celan; as demanded by a recalcitrant book ('Ars Poetica with Poppies and Birds'); as a "*living flame of love*" in a poem from Romania, and intense but inhibited "mouths" in its English version ('Poppies in Translation'). However, simply to track this collection's declared themes misses its strangeness and its sometimes baffling variety and length.

Nevertheless, it is full of pleasure and sensuous precision. If Bhatt's lightly worn knowledge of language, place and culture (so many poets name-checked or referred to) might be daunting, the poems remain resolutely open to the reader. A dash may act as the closing punctuation mark for a poem or stanza, and the frequent first or second person address welcomes the reader. So, too, do Bhatt's constant questions, which can be surreal, informative, tricksy, delighted – or pure flourish. And sometimes the trademark interrogative simply pays homage to pity: "What can I say?" ('Straight Through the Heart').

Some of the narratives were high points for me – 'A Secret', '*Viriditas*: Hildegard and Jesus', 'Florence' (fallout from the sending of an ill-considered postcard) and 'Faux Fable, with Butterfly'. The latter two poems share a sense of being parables of female knowingness: "everyone speaks of the lake instead, / not knowing that the lake is an ornament" ('Faux Fable, with Butterfly'). The poems of place and family memory sensitively draw past into present in 'At First She Was a Butterfly', 'Reading Sappho, I Am Reminded of Chickpeas' or 'Old Love Never Rusts'.

There is modesty in a poem's claim to be simply overhearing ("It is the lovers who call their words dark – / Not me – I merely try to listen – / I merely try to follow their story" ('*Schlafmohn, Blaumohn: Allerleilustblume*'). Bhatt's careful listening brings her many stories, of which perhaps the most horrific is 'Straight Through the Heart', where a bride's confession of being raped ten years previously triggers her murder. Earlier knowledge had been hidden or smoothed over in 'A Witness', 'A Secret' and 'Achill' (in which an infant's bones found on a beach are re-buried), but it is this poem to which they seem to point, and where Bhatt, fittingly, has to abandon her featherlight technique even to tell the tale.

The poems vary in weight and effectiveness and occasionally the surrealism and non sequiturs feel capricious. The last section (inspired by phrases in a Japanese-German grammar book) was less successful, though several poems display a subtle balance between normality and crisis.

. . .

Selima Hill is at least as much a one-off, if a more inward one. *Jutland* contains two sequences of fierce miniature poems that flirt with disaster, violence, disorder and the claims of pity and love: 'Advice on Wearing Animal Prints' (whose twenty-six poems, 'A' to 'Z', originally appeared as a Flarestack pamphlet), and the longer 'Sunday Afternoons at the Gravel-pits'.

These poems are as definite as the hard-bodied and violent girls of the gravel-pits but, like them, are "nowhere near as hard as you might think" ('Mahogany'), tottering on the edges of fury and forgiveness. Perspectives shift and rebels become vulnerable in Hill's expertly controlled segmented fictions.

A characteristic utterance in 'Animal Prints' is a strange tonal chime of exclamation: "There's still a nasty scar and no one knows / he didn't get it *surfing in Hawaii!*" ('S'); or "The older girls like bouncing on her face!" ('F'). The sequence compels the reader through Agatha's strange transformation, the give-and-take of abuse – kickings especially – and past deteriorating animals with their peculiar smells. For all her spirit, Agatha ends up "lying on the floor as good as gold", with "no breath" ('X').

'Sunday Afternoons at the Gravel-pits' is less bizarre but no less electric, reading as a daughter's reconstruction of an unloved father, exploring the potential for forgiveness after his death. The effect is somewhat strobe-like, with tiny metonyms for the father ('My Father's Chair' / 'Canary' / 'Tin' / 'Swimming Trunks') coming into momentary, brightly lit focus. A reader becomes oddly alert for small clues as each poem flashes up, one more key to a syncopated story, recomposed on each reading.

Hill's individual use of blatant simile is well known, her comparisons weird but strangely communicative. 'My Father's Knees' grip the speaker "like the guards of a palace / inhabited by moths made of gold-dust". She does as she pleases, sometimes discarding the tenor and travelling on in the vehicle for the rest of the poem, as in 'My Stiff Organza', where the speaker's body "quivers like a body made of snails // that live apart inside a snail city / that's not so much a city as an aerodrome [...]". Another pleasure is how often, in a four-line poem, she manages to surprise, her sentences mischieviously delaying the release of key information:

> First of all I will forget the tongue,
> and secondly I will forget the mouth;

and then I will forget the room itself
in which he would secrete me like a cheese.
('Tongue')

Abstractions (forgiveness, love, fear, shame) crowd the sequence's close and may deprive it of its earlier dazzle, but there's a satisfaction in the near-conclusion. Perhaps 'Hope' and 'My Father's Daughter' feel almost too mirrored, but the end, like pretty much everything in this sequence, is perfect. When the speaker thinks she sees her dead father, she feels her "heart go out to him" when "I saw him, or I thought I saw him, shiver, / as if he were a pool or a whippet" ('Although Of Course I Know He Isn't Here').

...

There's a vivid Stephen King-style underness to the Suffolk coast in Blake Morrison's 'The Ballad of Shingle Street', which is like King's Maine in its double nature. Jaunty down-home rhyming coexists with horror once you start to dig below the oven-warm stones to "smell the oil and taste the fear". The linkage between human events and natural and political threats is swiftly established. In 'On the Beach', there's "a row of pebbles stuck to your back / like medals awarded for bravery", giving a foretaste of war, injury and displacement to come.

The collection describes a themed arc, elegantly but never doggedly. It travels from sinister sea coast (where the supernatural supplements the dangers of coastal erosion and tidal wave) via a few salty, but often threatened erotics, to holiday nostalgia, elegy and the speaker's own mortality. The collection closes with a series of dying falls that recall Larkin: "Brief heat. Then death. That is the law" ('Harvest') and "the track and field events are over for the day [...]" ('Latecomer').

A significant swerve comes in the powerfully long-lined and game-changing 'Wave', which makes several of the book's themes explicit:

[...] wouldn't wipeout in an instant
be better than this slow deletion, as the sea rises and the cliffs are
beaten back,

and you receding in step, your bones thinning, your hair whitening,
and the thing that will kill you already triggered and on the move [...]

'This Poem...' offers an interlude, the sequence playing topical variations on a single conceit to talk about surveillance, corporate life and cover-up, with varying levels of subtlety. 'Hacking', 'Prism' and 'Inappropriate', where vested interests colonise the poem's (and the reader's) hitherto private space, work particularly well.

There's a serene confidence here, nearly thirty years on from Morrison's 1987 *The Ballad of the Yorkshire Ripper and other poems*. The textures are quieter, and more spacious, though Morrison still hovers skilfully over his issues like a bravura cursor, ringing one more change than you expected, still looking through a concerned lens at "our island" and unable to resist a few lists. It's a smooth, humane performance though very occasionally some of the elegiac moves feel a little standard. Morrison pre-empts this charge, opening the last poem, 'Latecomer', with: 'All I'm saying has been said before, but not by me." Similarly, if colloquial personification features a little too often in the coast's erosion (the wheat is "living on the edge", waves "live it up", the sea "flounces in", the cliffs "backed away, / abashed by the ocean's passion"), the last line of 'Sea Walk' finally pushes this device to its risky limit and redeems it: "The trees look scared to death."

Most of Morrison's last lines are absolutely in charge. There are occasional points where poems – or the ends of certain poems – seem a little flimsy or flat ("the music of eternity" in 'Anglers'), but it is rarer for them to explode into real unexpectedness. However, this is a smart and skilled book, knowing how little to say, and fully in control. The way in which its concerns take centre stage in these clean, surefooted poems, is moving and impressive.

Judy Brown's Loudness *is published by Seren. Her second collection is due in 2016.*

RIVERS OF TIME

Paul Henry, Boy Running, *Seren, £9.99*
ISBN 9781781722268
Anthony Howell, Silent Highway, *Anvil, £10.95*
ISBN 9780856464522
Gerry Murphy, Muse, *Dedalus, €11.50*
ISBN 9781910251058

reviewed by Fiona Moore

. . .

"So we've moved out of the years" – the first line from 'Usk', the opening poem in Paul Henry's sixth collection, *Boy Running*, stands well for what he does: shift time, space and categories to bring the reader into a dream-like state. Henry is working at the core of lyric poetry, with love and loss and the "deeper river",

> [...] listening to its quieter turns
>
> to the voices of loved ones
> you thought would never rise again,
> holding you now, with an old refrain.
> Under the river a deeper river runs.
>
> ('Under the River')

That passage is typically fluid in its movement, sustained partly by the echoing sound effects of the end-rhymes and repetitions of -old, -un-, trochaic -er words, and vs. No surprise that this poet is also a singer-songwriter. His many declaratory first lines feel song-like – see 'Usk' and the last line of 'Under the River', which is also that poem's first. There's striking imagery, too. Regrets for a lost marriage are summed up in a five-line poem, 'Ring': "I can't get the ring out of my finger". The "out of" is typical – the way Henry plays with time and prepositions has a trace of W.S. Graham.

Those quotations are from the book's first and longest section, which is full of personal reflections. The speaker's voice feels close to the reader, almost at her ear (Graham again). It recedes a little in the final section, which centres on Davy Blackrock, a modern, lonely, ageing singer-songwriter. Behind the poems lies the story of eighteenth-century Welsh bard Dafydd of the White Rock, who died young. So: what if Dafydd had died old and today, what fate might await the author? I didn't find this series quite as compelling, perhaps because Henry is projecting forward rather than mining the past. Perhaps he does deeply personal lyric best. Occasionally, the images feel generic when not taking off from something concrete: "He will ghost through the night / as water over stone" ('Blackrock Asleep'). But there's some nicely gritty urban detail to contrast with the more rural first section. Satellite dishes are "begging bowls / in the rain" ('Davy Blackrock'). And there's a lovely, ballad-like 'Song of a Wire Fence' about unfulfilled love.

The middle section consists mostly of a longer poem, 'Kicking the Stone'. This recreates a 60s housing estate and its ghosts, through which a boy kicks an autobiographical and four-million-year-old stone:

> Coming down from the Clay's
> Whistling Alan passes through me
> and the stone I kick
> passes through Whistling Alan.

It's a nice conceit that borders on the whimsical. There's something of Llareggub in the dottiness, without Dylan Thomas's extravagance of language, and also something of his *A Child's Christmas in Wales*.

I'll go back to *Boy Running* to immerse myself in the first section's layers of deeper river and for moments like this from 'Studio Flat':

> What's an attic
> but a bungalow in the sky.

There's a river running through the second section of Anthony Howell's *Silent Highway*, but a very different one: the Thames, overflowing with not-at-all-silent history. These poems are packed with research, from Gog and Magog to the *Marchioness* disaster; some bristle with capital letters. Much of the detail is absorbing, though it can risk overwhelming the poetry. Written in a variety of forms and in styles that range from the low-key to the mock-heroic ("Apotheosis! Arsenals of the sky / Ablaze" is how the sequence starts), the poems work best when Howell deploys his facility with rhythm and rhyme. Part of 'Windrush' is in the voice of a Jamaican whose Spitfire pilot father never returned from the war:

> When Mr Harold Wilson make a bonfire of Controls
> We come to Great Britain to repair their holes.
>
> And when me see the chimneys ranged along the shore
> Me say with all them factories no one can be poor.

The next part contains a long and fascinating passage on Thames thieves from mudlarks to "heavy horsemen" who

> [...] generally went furnished with habiliments
> designed to hide all manner of commodities:
> Sugar, coffee, cocoa and pimento,
> carried on shore by means of an under waistcoat
>
> Harbouring pockets all round, and also
> surreptitious bags, pouches, socks
> Tied to their midriffs underneath their trowsers.

Many poems in the rest of the book convey a sense of ennui. As with the river sequence, the more memorable have a clear rhythm and/or rhyme scheme – such as 'The Deserted Garage', which has long, rhyming lines: "that rusted compressor / Lying on one bent and eroded support like some defunct grass-hopper". This comes from the book's third section, 'Seeing Myself', which is full of landscapes that are edgelands or have an edgeland feel, or contain an edgeland relationship ('Tryst in a Suburb'). The women who appear here and there tend to be somewhat objectified. A poem that stands out is 'Seeing Myself', a nine-liner at the end of this section. It allows the reader more imaginative space than much of *Silent Highway*. It outlines, very lightly, a boy flicking stones at the sea, stones "Used by the sea already, those that fit".

Reading Gerry Murphy's *Muse* is like listening to one long shaggy-dog story in the pub; the amiable speaker addresses love, religion, life, death and so on in one anecdotal poem after another. Long and thin or short and thin, these fall fluently down the page. At their best, they are charming and/or funny and show a deft touch. The title poem opens the book with the speaker "writing naked" when his girlfriend comes out of the shower:

> A few drops from
> your dripping hair
> splash onto the lamp-lit page,
> blurring the words
> I am deploying in your honour.

So he has to begin again. There's a trace of Thomas Wyatt's 'They flee from me' in here: "you steal in... you slip". In a few love poems the male gaze gets a bit heavy and tends towards cliché, as in 'Train to Sligo', which contains "pert kissable breasts" and disapproving nuns. Having a go at religion is more fun in 'Romp', which describes what students high on dope can do with white paint:

> We started with the usual slogans:
> "Smash The State" on our own back gate
> ...
> "Strangle The Druids With Their Own Entrails"
> on the Chaplain's Notice Board

The slogans' escalating wackiness gives the poem energy. Yet there's a sadness to it, a sense of whistling-in-the-dark – it's in memory of (presumably) a fellow sloganeer. That sense recurs throughout the book.

As with any shaggy dog story, there are parts that may make the listener go *so what?* For example, the pilot of a plunging F-16 regresses to a baby in the cockpit as his life flashes past (I felt it didn't quite come off); a president arrives in the middle of nowhere. Murphy handles his chosen form skilfully, though its minor drawbacks become apparent after reading several thin poems in a row. Line breaks mostly run with the sense, which can make the line endings feel heavy, and not all the shortest lines stand up. Every now and then there's a wider poem, a welcome contrast.

Pleasures include a nice small poem, 'Tractor' (after Karen Solie – one of several 'after X' poems), whose monstrously expensive subject is "Possessed of the ecology / of a small tropical island", and another about a broadcast of the first moon landing degrading as it plays ever further out in space. 'Parallel Universe' describes stopping off at a corrugated-iron shop "with its rows of sweet jars, throbbing fridge, / obscure agricultural products" on a cycling trip that turns into a ghost story, and delivers a satisfying moment of chill. The chief enjoyments of *Muse* lie in its best poems and in the process of going with the flow, wondering whatever will come next.

Fiona Moore's pamphlet The Only Reason for Time *was published by HappenStance in 2013.*

FINELY GRAINED AMBIVALENCE

J.H. Prynne, Poems, *Bloodaxe, £25*
ISBN 9781780371542

reviewed by Patrick Mackie

...

The scale of the achievement strikes us first, and then comes a uneasy but genuine gratitude at the levels of ambition and commitment that have gone into the life's work gathered in this volume. Prynne's *Poems* as we have it now is in its third iteration, following the versions of 1999 and of 2005, which gathered together the various limbs of his oeuvre from their notoriously elusive berths, mainly in small-press or boutique editions. So this version adds the contents of five small volumes published since the last *Poems*, along with seven miscellaneous pieces. Readers are thus asked to purchase a suavely hefty and quietly expensive book for the sake of these slippery additions. Of course, the motive for this is unlikely to be raw commerce. Rather, a claim is staked as to the unity and even the monumentality of what Prynne has been up to for more or less half a century. The book is meant to be both a landmark, leaving us in no doubt as to his importance, and an immersion whereby all the poems gather meanings and refractions and momentums from one another. It would be nice to be as awestruck as the book seems to feel that we should be. Perhaps it would be nice, too, if we could simply feel, instead, that Prynne needs tearing down or crossing off, and that the plentiful detractors of his burning brand of pushy experimentation were right all along. But, in truth, it is ambivalence that the book finally provokes.

So the question becomes one of the quality of this ambivalence, of how hard the book pulls our responses in two different directions. It is not just that ambivalence is not the same thing as indifference; it may be that the richest or most finely grained ambivalence is the opposite of the latter. Likewise, it will be worth wondering what it is that these poems are themselves most ambivalent about. The present volume makes available for comparative inspection the expansive range of options that Prynne's commitment to poetic experiment has meant, and what this, accumulatingly, makes us realise is how uncertain his best work has been about the shapes that such experiment should assume, and even about the validity of what experiment he has been capable of. So we have at the head of the volume the aphoristic intellectual pushiness of 1968's *Kitchen Poems*, but then dated to the following year comes *The White Stones*, a collection that opens back on to a more ample and tonally varied lyricism and permits itself a more playful stance towards its own argumentative drives. During the 1970s we find the flickery and diaristic *Into the Day*, but also the more pre-emptively hemmed-in and moodily minimalised sequence *The Land of Saint Martin*. By the 1990s, the vibrancy of these oscillations seems to have slackened, and collections such as *Her Weasels Wild Returning* and *Pearls That Were* become far more stylistically homogenous than the variety of shapes made by their poems on the page would suggest. Prynne's increasing addiction to parataxis is a big part of this slide into something much like a stylistic system. Earlier works had featured more playful and nimble fusions of parataxis with variously expanded or cauterised, and in fact sometimes archly strict, versions of conventional syntax. Prynne's admirers seem often to have wanted him to be the emperor of experiment, permitted to doubt everything except the sway of his own subversions. We may wonder whether, by this point, he had not become stuck in the poses of a vision of restlessness so fully assumed as to become paralysing itself.

Consider a poem from Prynne's 1969 volume, 'Quality in that Case as Pressure', in which he amply writes that "How *much* we / see is how much we desire change", and with moving openness describes being "moved / by the *condition* of knowledge". Using italics is one way of conjuring the pressure of a real and desirous voice within the density of the poem's movement. Likewise, we believe his rhapsodic and fissured account there of a sunset as part of "the oblique / turned into a great torque which is / pleasure", because there is already so much pleasure in the conflations of obliquity with plainness in his phrasing and syntax. The poem goes on to test this painstakingly considered version of rapture with darting and testy little thoughts on economics or minerals or what it calls ethical frenzy. But the point is it was developing from the start a style nimble enough to play these elements off against each other, one capable of holding rapture and destructive speculation in a single linguistic gesture. Now consider this sentence from the 1998 sequence *Red D Gypsum*, in which Prynne sought a vociferously reinvented version of landscape poetry:

> Attrapment bezels stir up the current fissure relented
> to a chimney of yellow powder.

We do sort of see what he means, and there is indeed something mimetically suited to the experience of walking about the crushing together here of physiognomic detail with slightly arch bursts of knowledge or metaphor. But if we then consider another sentence from later in the sequence, we begin to gauge how repetitive or indeed rutted the trick becomes:

> Newly
> marine devices glimmer at a bark scripture advented
> dyestuff.

The metonymic play is never less than apt and suggestive, and the shunting together of bark and scripture is no doubt something any bookish type who goes for walks will receive as experientially actual. But the voice has lost its give and variousness, and hence its capacity to weigh experience acutely. When we get to the "moiety report preventing / issuance to bind over thin var faction" in the 2004 *Blue Slides at Rest* sequence, or to the "placard of renewed angular motion" a few pages later, the sense of an almost comically relentless machine for pressing out phrases becomes hard to ignore. Far from the wayfaring experimenter restlessly trying out new forms, Prynne comes close to his own idiosyncratic and tortuous Parnassian in such poems.

No doubt the combinations of neglect and adulation visited on Prynne have made his trajectory peculiarly uncanny. It is tempting to report either that the emperor has all the flashy regalia anyone could claim or that he is stunningly naked. Something in the project of the artistic avant-garde, generally, pushes towards such extreme options, and involves us in a pre-emptive radicalisation of aesthetic judgement; a readymade by Duchamp and a piece of electronica by Stockhausen alike dare us to think they are either masterpieces or nonsense. But with Prynne the twist is he has remained so divisive even while his poems have failed to sustain this dilemma in its original sharpness. Far too many poems in the second half of the book, in particular, are more like photocopies of some fading experimental impulse. The drastic complexity of surface starts to feel botched all too wilfully, and the underlying shapes to feel prefabricated. Simpler models of experience replace such textured conflicts as the one between a wheelingly expansive Lucretian pessimism and a sweetly traditional English pastoralism that positively forced his earlier landscape poems into experimentation. Maybe he ended up figuring out exactly what he thinks about too many different things for his poems to stay pungent. At times, his impasse resembles Auden's, who also could not finally work out how to push forward the inheritances and dilemmas left by the glory years of modernism, and whose later poems, too, substitute easy intellectual virtuosity for the work of thought. The air of donnish preciousness that overwhelms us in the later Auden is perhaps only a whiff in Prynne, but it is unmistakably present by the time of his three books of *Triodes*, as their jokey protagonist Pandora wheels easily through world-historical reference points and all-too-polished shifts of perspective. The pathos of the fragmentary has lost its juice, and parataxis has become a shortcut to reminiscences of what real experiment enjoins. Doubtless, he has remained too uncompromising to be accused of having become a man of letters. But he has slipped closer to the good taste of the creative writing circuit and the London prize committees than many of his admirers want to think.

One problem with reissuing essentially the same book in expanded versions over the years is that the reception of Prynne's work ends up seeming to have been static in the decade and a half since the first volume. So, essentially the same reviews appear, hailing him as the unacknowledged master of the past few decades of British poetry, and explaining what are always taken to be the difficulty and rebarbativeness of his poems as consequences of the urgency and authenticity of his late modernist project. In some ways, these repetitions should reassure us. Fierce quantities of scholarly spadework have indeed been going on in the background, piecing together exegeses of the poems and elucidating their workings. But the overall account of his work has thus continued to be undiscriminating. Numerous calls have gone out for a mainstream readership to engage with him, but no one has tried to explain which of his poems this should involve, or how they should be presented and illuminated beyond a coterie readership. Likewise, endless restatements of how difficult he is have not encouraged awareness of how multivalent and slippery a concept difficulty is, how volatile an act it amounts to. But the trouble with much of Prynne's work is not that it is too difficult, but it is not difficult enough, or rather the idea of difficulty that underpins it is too easy or convenient for discomfort. His rebarbativeness, to certain readers, is ingratiation itself. Despite all the political animadversions his work sincerely and valiantly encodes, Prynne comes close to being the ideal poet of the neoliberal university.

Bloodaxe might have done better to have issued a selected volume culled from the previous iteration of *Poems*, alongside a book of late poems comprising the sections added at the end of this one. Of course, the poet's devotees would have thrown miffed accusations of reductiveness and distortion, and cried out mightily about whatever was excluded, but this would have been grist to the more energetic discussion that we need if his work is to become more widely alive. Let us not lose sight of our ambivalence amongst all these rather pushy reservations and recommendations; the book we have is in many ways wonderful, and it is splendidly presented. A separate presentation of the most recent material would have had the further advantage, however, of focusing attention on how distinctly and distinctively good parts it are. In particular, the long meditation *Kazoo Dreamboats; or, On What There Is* has a profuse but also nicely ragged amplitude that breathes new air into Prynne's style of dense connection. Likewise, the little lyrics in the booklet *Al-Dente* bear out that title's suggestion of not being overcooked, and generate a refined and whispy music out of precisely their own liberating modesty. Too often, over the course of the volume's second half at least, Prynne comes across as a late modernist equivalent of Swinburne, trapped in his own hectically obsessional vision of what poetry should be. But then the closing sections find him slipping free of the bear hug of his own idea of experimentation, and making new shapes again out of real needs and pleasures.

Patrick Mackie's second collection is due from CB editions in 2016.

LATE EXCELLENCE

Dannie Abse, Ask the Moon: New and Collected Poems 1948-2014
Hutchinson, £20, ISBN 9780091958916

reviewed by Alan Brownjohn

...

Dannie Abse had just passed his ninety-first birthday when he died at the end of September 2014. Despite his having reached that age the news came as a shock, except naturally for those closest to him. Only weeks before he had been bringing out poems and appearing in public, showing his usual energy and optimism. He had dispatched this big volume to the press earlier that month. Now it's published, we find that he had done a fresh author's note at the same time, citing some solemn thoughts on life and poetry from his much admired Rilke – and this did read like a kind of farewell, though the stress on 'New' in the book's subtitle could be read as allowing a hope for more to come, even yet.

Sadly that was not to be, so *Ask the Moon*, as well as offering, in the words of the publisher that has supported him loyally since his very first book, a "definitive collection of Dannie Abse's lifetime's work", therefore provides a resounding last statement of his faith in the art of poetry as a vehicle of "pleasure, comedy and grief" – as also of his confidence in the way in which he practised it, with both fun and seriousness, over six decades. Owners of all, or even a few, of the fourteen books from which he chooses poems here should certainly hold on to them, because some favourites will always be excluded by a poet's strange decisions (why, I wonder, omit the gripping variation on Rilke's 'Das Karussell' from *Ask the Bloody Horse*, 1986, or 'The Expert' from *Arcadia, One Mile*, 1998?). But in the end this is a splendidly comprehensive *Collected*, well produced except for needing a little more reader-friendly generosity in its spacing.

It is, in fact, Abse's fourth such compilation, the first *Collected Poems* having appeared in 1976 with work from five of his first six books. As an introduction to "a new and original poet", the unrepresented debut volume, *After Every Green Thing* (1948), which he wrote while still a medical student, only proved that it was quite possible to recover from a dreadful beginning. In his acknowledgements he thanked "Mr Edmund Blunden for his early encouragement and kindness". This would be unbelievable if one didn't know how generous with time and patience some poets can be, because there was no debt whatsoever to the saintly Blunden as a poet. There was a real one to Dylan Thomas, though not for any mastery of craft or structure. More dismally, the book (which he disowned later) relied on the chaotic imagery and vocabulary of 1940s neo-romantic poetry as practised by the 1940s 'Apocalyptic' movement. In 'Poem in November' (compare and contrast Thomas's 'Poem in October') we encounter, "Oh the leaves of music that scrape / the pavements seeking a softer grave. Oh the restless / wind walking through brown fog with blue hands / against the fractured lampposts." It is not clear how Abse managed to emerge from this dead end, retaining (and including here among 'Early Poems') only a couple of poems – a cryptic piece titled 'The Uninvited' and the very personal 'Epithalamium', to which he returned at readings all his life. But emerge he did, with remarkable speed, early in the next decade. Possibly that transformation came about through realising that a poem could be used to speak intimately and thoughtfully to a friend, in 'Letter to Alex Comfort'? Or in finding a vein of pointful humour in 'Letter to *The Times*'? Or discovering a talent for the grim ballad with 'The Trial', and a flair for classical narrative (and rhetorical cadences) with 'The Victim of Aulis'? All of these abilities are present in what he produced later. But however Abse achieved the change, what he established with the more disciplined form and calmer atmosphere of *Tenants of the House* (1957) and *Poems, Golders Green* (1962) was a style he never abandoned, a pattern for almost all his subsequent work.

He had finished his training and had been working as a doctor for some time before showing evidence in the poems of his day-to-day medical routine. 'Pathology of Colours' – colours can be deathly as well as beautiful – is from *A Small Desperation* (1968), his fifth book and the third represented here. By implication the poem suggests that the 'duality' in the successful life he leads as poet and hospital specialist, contriving to wear "white coat and purple coat" simultaneously, worries him and just has to be faced: "I know the colour rose, and it is lovely, / but not when it ripens in a tumour; / and healing greens, leaves and grass, so springlike, / in limbs that fester are not springlike." The abruptness of the confrontation is uneasy as well as harsh, and the reader might have wondered where Abse could go from there on this topic. But writing this poem seemed to take him over a border into a territory where he could bring a new candour and insight to subjects such as the Holocaust (in 'A Night Out') or family loss, as when he visits his dying father in 'In Llandough Hospital':

> I grasp his hand so fine, so mild,
> which still is warm surprisingly,
> not a handshake either, father,
> but as I used to when a child.

He can now bring into his poetry hospital scenes that have suddenly seized his attention, such as the observation of births in 'The Smile Was', or he can tell in verse the horrifying narrative of an operation witnessed by his brother in 'In the Theatre' – producing two of his most memorable poems. This effort culminates in 'Carnal Knowledge', from his 1989 volume *Remembrance of Crimes Past* – it may be significant that he didn't write it until then – which is surely one of the frankest and finest poems ever written by a doctor about his profession. When he has retired from medicine, the lucidity and honesty are transferred to his late – touching and vulnerable – poems of married love and bereavement, featured in the volume *Two for Joy* (2010). Newly exploring Welsh scenes and themes and dipping more deeply, if still keeping a somewhat sardonic distance, into Jewish lore and tradition, these poems brought a new variety into the work of his last years. It is hard to think of another poet, except possibly Thomas Hardy, who continued to write so prolifically – and so well – in his eighties.

What also arrived with the years of medical experience (and could it be attributed to it?) was a characteristic mode of delivery. In more instances than with most poets, Abse came at the reader with the first person singular ("I know the colour rose") and carried it off by deploying the warmth, clarity and economy required of a good doctor. He addressed his hearers on a one-to-one basis that sounded informal but carried authority. It was a skill that guaranteed the attention of audiences at many hundreds of readings, including a famous long series of Poetry and Jazz nights with famous artists. In his youth he scorned the 1950s Movement verse in which, "Proudly English ... no one dances, no one rejoices" ('Enter the Movement'). Yet while many of his own poems entertained, he never became the mere entertainer. He had a mission to communicate, in as measured and truthful – and comprehensible – a way as possible. So numerous poems that at first seemed easy of access, and earned him praise for wearing his humanity lightly, unexpectedly acquire a greater power and depth on the page and deserve not to be underestimated – 'Hunt the Thimble', 'Encounter at a Greyhound Bus Station' and 'Rilke's Confession' are examples from three different periods. All at once these seem out of place beside the lighter (sometimes even embarrassing) items Abse was determined to keep. His *New and Collected Poems* can, and should, be read now for the pleasure given by the calm, humane, good-humoured voice that has just fallen silent. But it should be retained for the darker, more insightful poems that will most surely last.

Alan Brownjohn's The Saner Places: Selected Poems *is published by Enitharmon.*

THE GEOFFREY DEARMER PRIZE 2014

Judge: Bill Manhire

I read forty poems by nineteen writers, and pretty impressive they all were. Lucky for me I wasn't asked to find a shortlist, as that might have been even harder than settling on a single winner. Part of my problem would have been that, where a couple of decades ago English poetry consisted of a well-formed, meandering mainstream (plus some smaller, wilder, quite separate waterways), it now looks more like a braided river, with many shifting and interweaving channels.

Anyway, my Geoffrey Dearmer winner is Zaffar Kunial for his three poems – 'The Word', 'Q' and 'Fielder' – which appeared in issue 104:3 of *The Poetry Review*. I like the way they deal with the difficulties of identity and orientation without becoming noisily theatrical or, worse, complacent. A poem such as 'The Word' is deftly made. You notice fairly soon that it's a sonnet with a rusty hinge in the middle (a diptych then?), presumably there to make visible the "two minds" that the poem describes. Likewise, the way the poem rides on its half rhymes captures the "half right, half / wrong" place to which the text finds its way.

To mention such formal pleasures is perhaps to imply that 'The Word' is an over-managed piece of writing – tidy, pre-determined, just a bit too settled in its understandings. But that's not the effect at all. Kunial's voice is quiet, hesitating, tongue-tied even. His poems' intellectual and emotional positions are, I suppose, 'post-colonial' – "beyond the boundary, / in [the] edgeland of central England", as 'Fielder' puts it, but the writer I'm most reminded of is Thomas Hardy. As with Hardy, awkwardness grants a kind of calming grace to difficult contemplation. A very different poet, Anne Carson, says that "a page with a poem on it is less attractive than a page with a poem on it and some tea stains" – and that's perhaps another way of explaining why I have chosen Kunial's poems for this award.

Bill Manhire's Selected Poems *is published by Carcanet.*

ZAFFAR KUNIAL

The Word

I couldn't tell you now what possessed me
to shut summer out and stay in my room.
Or at least attempt to. In bed mostly.
It's my dad, standing in the door frame
not entering – but pausing to shape advice
that keeps coming back. "Whatever is matter,

must *enjoy the life*." He pronounced this twice.
And me, I heard wrongness in putting a *the*

before *life*. In two minds. Ashamed. Aware.
That I knew better, though was stuck inside
while the sun was out. That I'm native here.
In a halfway house. Like that sticking word.
That definite article, half right, half
wrong, still present between *enjoy* and *life*.

First published in The Poetry Review, *104:3, Autumn 2014.*

Jane Austen: Selected Letters

Where shall I begin? she starts. *Which of all*
my important nothings shall I tell you first?
In her shortened sign-off, above, she'd *remain*
with Love,
            Yrs affec JA.
And I'm reading names into the absences;
Julia Ann... who helped my initial scribbles
and kept an old card with first words in my hand:

from Zaffar
            – the *ff* pointing backwards,
back to that consonant I couldn't then say;
stuck with my start, I was an Affer, or Faffer –
which proved true, Mum later said, of the latter.
Dawdler that I became. So here I am

taken aback by letters – their afterlife –
and how we draw together when they arrive.

. . .

We also talk of a Laburnam. – The Border
under the Terrace Wall is clearing away...

I go back and look at that second a
in *Laburnam*. It's you, Mum, I remember
explaining to me how a soft Indian u
is equally an a. My dad taught me to say
'Mera nam Zaffar hai'. The first vowel
in my name like the last u in laburnum.

As a child I'd climb that tree, spend hours lost in
its grey-green limbs at the end of our garden.

Early days, at the registry, in Birmingham
Mum wrote out, in her own spelling... *Kunial*
from Jatrajputkanyal – Dad's tribe or clan,
clearing the part that talked of caste.
                                        In *Austen*
that A, almost from the off, is a different sound –
more like the o in of, than the u in ground.

Zaffar Kunial *published a pamphlet in the Faber New Poets series in 2014. He won third prize in the National Poetry Competition 2011 with 'Hill Speak'. In 2014, he became Poet-in-Residence at the Wordsworth Trust. He has contributed (with Steve Ely, Denise Riley and Warsan Shire) to* The Pity, *a series of new poems commissioned and published by the Poetry Society as a response to the centenary of the First World War.*

The Geoffrey Dearmer Prize *is awarded annually to the best poem in* The Poetry Review *by a poet who had not, at the time their work appeared, published a collection. It is funded through the generosity of the Dearmer family in honour of the poet Geoffrey Dearmer, who was a Poetry Society member.*

Letter from San Francisco

BRINGERS OF SONG

D.A. Powell

> *Sammy, the toucan, is fine – a neighbor built him a very large cage in which he seems quite happy, and I give him baths with the garden hose. Someone also brought him a big pair of gold earrings from the Petropolis 'Lojas Americana' (5 & 10) and he loves them. He has two noises – one a sort of low rattle in his throat, quite gentle, if he is pleased with you, or cranky, if he isn't, and the other, I'm afraid, a* shriek.
>
> *– Elizabeth Bishop, letter to Marianne Moore, from Brazil, 13 March 1952*

We have a word in California for someone who carries an umbrella: optimist.

I, like many poets before, believe the birds control the weather. In the order of heavenly beings, angels are lowest, therefore fit to act as messengers to humanity. Also teachers, with good and bad results. Angels are said to have taught us all kinds of things. But what of other things with wings? Do they not mimic the orders above them? Suspended on that most subtle element, the air, birds trace out the shifts and whims of winds, and they are the keepers of weather knowledge we cannot measure in such detail as those that measure with a feather. Climatic turns are adumbrated by them all the time if we but care to listen. Certainly we heed at least one canary, if only the one in the proverbial mineshaft.

Listen to the birds. I guess I don't have to tell that to poets. Poe's raven and Dunbar's turkey and Hopkins's windhover and Dickinson's bobolink and Yeats's falcon. If a bird's going to talk, it's going to talk to a poet. I don't know any other people who converse with nightingales. But don't just listen to their tunes: study them.

Much of the ancient art of augury centred on birds: their songs and their flight. Associations were perhaps based in superstition at times: an owl means death, for example. But one can imagine that the presence of an owl also signalled the presence of rodents, and perhaps a general descent into decay was detected in the owl's presence. But even if we admit that the meaning of an owl is not so cut and dried, there are plenty of ways in which we can tell a lot about people by the birds they keep company with. Falcons are for hunters. Eagles are for warriors. Flamingos. Ah, flamingos. They are for flames. People who light up a room. Hummingbirds are for industrious people or those with numerous interests.

Once a week, I put out a little seed for the sparrows who live in the mayten tree down below my front window. The couple use my fire escape for their cooling-off spot. They also bring their fledged youngsters and I have been witness to a couple of bird tragedies. But generally they are happy birds and the male, a white-capped sparrow, has a strong whistling morning song that tells me there's been some accumulation of moisture on the leaves of the hyssop or upon the flowers of the nasturtiums popping out red and gold. These are also a favorite of hummingbirds who stray over from the dense dells and find they need a pick-me-up. I can't lay out too much seed for the sparrows, as it'll draw the black-headed Steller's jays; they are a nuisance once they've got you marked, and they keep the sparrows away, which is not what I want. I want the sparrows to flourish. They are the simple bringers of song. Like poets, they are content to try the air all day with their voices, if the other birds will just let them alone.

And when the weather's bad, they hunker down, those nut-brown sparrows, chittering while the wind shakes their nest below. We are glad of sparrows – I mean, us, as humans, are comforted by sparrow songs. At the end of a day, the sparrow's downward whistle sounds like letting off steam, like letting out air. We all need that. Poetry does that, also: lets out air.

St Francis, famously, ministered to the birds: "It is God who made you noble among creatures, making your home in thin, pure air." He was convinced that their place in creation was close to heaven, and he made them to sing in praise of the Creator. In San Francisco, a city named for St Francis, sharp-shinned hawks hunt oscines, and red-winged blackbirds skim the ditches and ponds for mosquitos. At the shoreline, petrels, gulls and frigate birds sculpt the ocean's microsystem of waves and currents with their flight. In open areas where human traffic is high and discarded bits of sandwich or loose snack foods fall or are tossed away, grey pigeons, aggressive grackles, jays, blueblack crows and even tiny nuthatches will congregate and await the spoils of lunch. But these are usual suspects. Birds one hardly notices, even close at hand. We're accustomed to their presence. But we are dazzled by the newcomers: feral parrots, once confined mainly to a small area of North Beach, are being spotted in larger numbers; from Pacific Heights to the Twin Peaks, these exotics fly over the city, fanning their green, red and blue bodies in chevron-shaped flocks that chatter endlessly as they go in search of loquat trees or hawthorn berries. They are, like so many of us here, escapees. San Francisco is their refuge, and they are adapting to its moderate climate, we think. But perhaps we've got it wrong. Perhaps the climate of moderation and openness is brought by the birds themselves. Parrots open us to the unexpected. They are social, loud and showy, like the locals. And perhaps they are telling us: adapt, adapt, adapt.

I love Flaubert's short story 'A Simple Heart'. Felicity, a maid devoted to others, winds up with no one in her life except a stuffed parrot. Most people read this as sad. But not Felicity herself. She takes the parrot's presence as a sign of God's grace. And so at last, "when she breathed her last breath she thought she saw in the heavens as they opened, a gigantic parrot, flying above her head". She has been blessed by the presence of her totem bird, just as Mary is blessed by the dove.

Sure, bad messages can come from birds, too. Noah gets a bad report from the raven. As does Poe. And it is a dire report indeed from Yeats's falcon, which by its flight suggests that "the centre cannot hold". Perhaps the key is to cultivate relationships with friendly avians such as parrots. The ancient Roman augurs kept chickens on hand and took as a favourable sign the chicken's appetite for grains of wheat. When I see parrots in my neighbourhood, I take it as a sign of hope: the world goes on.

Gather to you the birds that signal happiness. That might mean opening a waterway or building a pond. It might be just finding the right spot to put a feeder. Tend to making a world that welcomes wild song. When the birds come, they will bring word of how to live and what to write down.

LETTER TO THE EDITOR

A fight to the death by villanelle

Dear Editor,

It was a pleasure to be guided through the poetry of Michael Donaghy, as well as Don Paterson's accompanying critical guide to the late poet's work, by the adroit and assured hand of Jack Underwood in the previous issue of *The Poetry Review* ['Mirror-within-mirror', review essay: TPR 105:1]. In his lively and smart critique I found plenty to provoke, not least discussion of the American's peculiarly heightened awareness of poetry's emotional import, coupled with its inescapable artifice.

In the company of a capable reviewer, then, how baffling to find an obtuse dismissal of those who might, on one level, admire the formal panache of Donaghy's poems. "The fetishism of certain technical qualities in Donaghy's work feel[s] a bit like someone explaining the benefits of power steering in the Mondeo", Underwood quips. But lest we miss the point amid the self-delighted wit, such a statement in fact implies that, just as all contemporary cars are equipped with the tech to help negotiate a tight parallel park, all contemporary poets are in possession of the poetic craft that makes a poem truly memorable, and memorisable. Underwood goes on to separate Donaghy from those "contemporaries whom one can still occasionally find earnestly aerobicising their iambs in macho displays of supposed subtlety and control". Showy formalism for formalism's sake is a poor impersonation of deft and purposeful use of form. But the defensive smugness of tone here is strange – as is the suggestion that anything related to the art of poesy might be considered "macho" by anyone. Forget that arm-wrestle in the pub. It's a fight to the death by villanelle that'll sort the men from the boys.

Ben Wilkinson
Sheffield, South Yorkshire

CONTRIBUTORS

Caroline Bird's most recent collection is *The Hat-Stand Union* (Carcanet, 2013) • **Miles Burrows** has won several awards in the Hippocrates Prize for Poetry and Medicine • **Geraldine Clarkson** is the winner of the *Magma* Editors' Prize 2015 • **Jamie Coward**'s debut pamphlet, *Peasholm Park*, is forthcoming from Mews Press. He lives in Sheffield • **Philip Gross**'s *The Love Songs of Carbon* is forthcoming from Bloodaxe in September • **Stephen Knight**'s most recent book is *The Prince of Wails* (CB editions, 2012) • **Jennifer L. Knox**'s *Days of Shame and Failure* is forthcoming from Bloof Books in September • **Nick Laird**'s third collection, *Go Giants* (Faber), was published in 2013 • **Gregory Leadbetter**'s pamphlet *The Body in the Well* was published by HappenStance in 2007 • **Frances Leviston**'s second collection, *Disinformation*, is published by Picador • **Ian McDonough** has been published extensively in periodicals. He lives in Edinburgh • **Graham Mort**'s *Visibility: New and Selected Poems* was published by Seren in 2007 • **Daljit Nagra**'s most recent collection is a version of the *Ramayana* (Faber, 2013) • **Alice Oswald**'s most recent collection is *Memorial* (Faber, 2011) • **Stephen Payne**'s first collection, *Pattern Beyond Chance*, will be published by HappenStance later this year • **Sara Peters**'s first collection, *1996*, was published by Anansi Press in 2013. She was born in Nova Scotia and lives in Toronto • **D.A. Powell**'s most recent collection is *Repast* (Graywolf, 2014) • **Mary Robinson**'s debut collection, *The Art of Gardening*, was published by Flambard in 2010 • **Amali Rodrigo**'s first collection is forthcoming from Bloodaxe in 2016 • **Laura Scott**'s pamphlet *What I Saw* was published by Rialto in 2013. She lives in Norwich • **F.J. Williams**'s *The Model Shop* was published by Waterloo Press in 2011 • **Jack Underwood**'s debut collection, *Happiness*, is published by Faber in July.

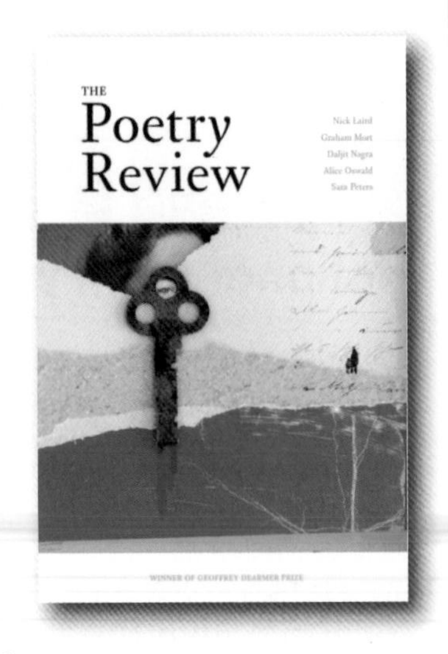
THE
Poetry
Review

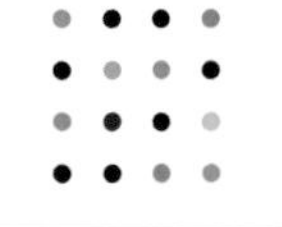